OXFORD WORLD'S CLASSICS

ON THE GENEALOGY OF MORALS

FRIEDRICH NIETZSCHE (1844–1900) was born in Röcken, Saxony, and educated at the universities of Bonn and Leipzig. After a precocious start to an academic career which saw him elected to a professorship at the University of Basle at the age of 25, he was forced to resign completely from his post in 1879 due to prolonged bouts of ill health. From then on he devoted himself entirely to thinking and writing. His early books and pamphlets (*The Birth of Tragedy*, *Untimely Meditations*) were heavily influenced by Wagner and Schopenhauer, but from *Human, All Too Human* (1878) on, his thought began to develop more independently, culminating in the prolific production of the late 1880s. In early 1889 Nietzsche suffered a mental breakdown from which he was never to recover. He died in Weimar in 1900. *On the Genealogy of Morals* (1887) is one of his most important books, a sustained critique of Christian and liberal ethics which provides an insight into the central preoccupation of his mature thought.

DOUGLAS SMITH is College Lecturer in French at University College, Dublin. Author of *Transvaluations: Nietzsche in France 1872–1972* (Clarendon Press, 1996), he has also translated *The Birth of Tragedy* for Oxford World's Classics.

OXFORD WORLD'S CLASSICS

For over 100 years Oxford World's Classics have brought readers closer to the world's great literature. Now with over 700 titles—from the 4,000-year-old myths of Mesopotamia to the twentieth century's greatest novels—the series makes available lesser-known as well as celebrated writing.

The pocket-sized hardbacks of the early years contained introductions by Virginia Woolf, T. S. Eliot, Graham Greene, and other literary figures which enriched the experience of reading. Today the series is recognized for its fine scholarship and reliability in texts that span world literature, drama and poetry, religion, philosophy and politics. Each edition includes perceptive commentary and essential background information to meet the changing needs of readers.

OXFORD WORLD'S CLASSICS

FRIEDRICH NIETZSCHE

On the Genealogy of Morals

A Polemic

By way of clarification and
supplement to my last book
Beyond Good and Evil

Translated with an Introduction and Notes by
DOUGLAS SMITH

OXFORD
UNIVERSITY PRESS

Great Clarendon Street, Oxford OX2 6DP

Oxford University Press is a department of the University of Oxford.
It furthers the University's objective of excellence in research, scholarship,
and education by publishing worldwide in

Oxford New York

Athens Auckland Bangkok Bogotá Buenos Aires Cape Town
Chennai Dar es Salaam Delhi Florence Hong Kong Istanbul Karachi
Kolkata Kuala Lumpur Madrid Melbourne Mexico City Mumbai Nairobi
Paris São Paulo Shanghai Singapore Taipei Tokyo Toronto Warsaw

with associated companies in Berlin Ibadan

Oxford is a registered trade mark of Oxford University Press
in the UK and in certain other countries

Published in the United States
by Oxford University Press Inc., New York

First published as a World's Classics paperback 1996
Reissued as an Oxford World's Classics paperback 1998

British Library Cataloguing in Publication Data
Data available

Library of Congress Cataloging in Publication Data

Nietzsche, Friedrich Wilhelm, 1844–1900.
[Zur Genealogie der Moral. English]
On the genealogy of morals : a polemic : by way of clarification
and supplement to my last book, Beyond good and evil / Friedrich
Nietzsche; translated with an introduction and notes by Douglas Smith.
(Oxford world's classics)
Includes bibliographical references and index.
1. Ethics. I. Smith, Douglas, Dr. II. Title. III. Series.
B3313.Z73E5 1997 170—dc20 96–10755

ISBN 0–19–283617–X

7 9 10 8

Printed in Great Britain by
Clays Ltd, St Ives plc

CONTENTS

INTRODUCTION

Skin Deep: Nietzsche's Critique of Ethics

On The Genealogy of Morals is arguably, after *The Birth of Tragedy*, Nietzsche's best-known book. It is, as the title suggests, a book about the history of ethics but also, as the title omits to state but the Preface makes clear, a book about interpretation. In terms of Nietzsche's argument, these two subjects are inextricably intertwined. As a history of ethics, the *Genealogy* pursues two aims. First, it seeks to discredit what Nietzsche sees as the dominant moral values of his age. These are in essence the values of Judaeo-Christian ethics—justice, equality, compassion—as they have been inherited and secularized by the Enlightenment tradition. Secondly, the *Genealogy* sets out to discredit the Victorian scientific critique of these values undertaken by Utilitarian philosophy, associationist psychology, Social Darwinism, and exclusively fact-based historical study. Nietzsche challenges the original and absolute status claimed by Judaeo-Christian values by arguing that they are in fact the historical product of a violent struggle between two relative types of morality. Then he challenges the scientific critique of such values on the basis of its mis-recognition of the determining forces which have produced them. For Nietzsche, both the prevailing moral values and their scientific critique are, for all their appeals to transcendental authority, nothing more than local expressions of an omnipresent and immanent will to power, the ruthless vital force which animates all life and drives all human activity. In this sense, both conventional morality and its critique are skin deep, superficial disguises masking the operations of the will to power.

As an engagement with the history of ethics and its scientific critique, Nietzsche's dual argument is centrally concerned with the writing of history and the procedures employed for its interpretation. The questions of how historical narratives are constructed and to which ends and in the service of which interests are recurrent themes. The *Genealogy* consistently contests not only the accepted historical truths of the time but also the very notion of truth itself. For Nietzsche, the questioning of the value of truth is implicated in the questioning of moral values, since moral values characteristically seek to establish themselves as truths. Nietzsche's interest in ethics is an anthropological one, and terms such as 'morality' and 'morals' are used more or less neutrally to designate historically relative sets of values and beliefs, rather than absolute moral truths. His critical point of departure is, in this respect, the divorce of morality from truth. As a prerequisite to examining these and other aspects of Nietzsche's argument in greater detail, some consideration of the context of his ideas is necessary, in relation both to his own work and to that of his contemporaries.

Before the Genealogy

The *Genealogy* revisits a number of themes which first emerged in Nietzsche's work of the early 1870s. These include a consideration of the origin of cultural phenomena and a critique of contemporary approaches to the study and writing of history. A brief comparison between his earlier and later positions on these matters offers a useful insight into the development of his thought. In his first major work, *The Birth of Tragedy*, Nietzsche set himself two different goals. His first aim was to locate the origin of Greek tragedy in a compromise between what he called the Apollonian and the Dionysian poles of Greek culture. While Apollo represented the desire for containment and form, Dionysus symbolized excess and loss of identity. For Nietzsche, the two poles were associated with the arts of sculpture and music respectively. Tragedy sought to unify sculptural form with the exuberance of music. The second aim of *The Birth of Tragedy* was to provide a kind of manifesto for an as-yet non-existent movement of German cultural regeneration focused on the work of Richard Wagner. For Nietzsche, Wagner's operas presented a series of enabling myths which would inspire German culture to rise above its current mediocrity.

In pursuing both these aims, *The Birth of Tragedy* was concerned to locate a point of departure for cultural change.

The *Genealogy*, by way of contrast, is less concerned with origins conceived as single punctual events (birth) and more with origins understood as the complex intersection of a number of different and competing forces (genealogy). It is also much less sympathetic to the intellectual mentors whose influence is so marked in *The Birth of Tragedy*—Wagner and Arthur Schopenhauer. By the late 1880s Nietzsche is vehemently opposed to the Schopenhauerian idea, adopted by Wagner, that the highest expression of the human will is to be found in self-abnegation.

Another work from the early 1870s which anticipates Nietzsche's later ideas on history is the second *Untimely Meditation*, *On the Use and Disadvantage of History* (1874). Like the *Genealogy*, *On the Use and Disadvantage...* is concerned with history and historiography and their relations to life and culture. The early essay is essentially a polemic directed at what Nietzsche regarded as a destructively historicist trend in German culture, an obsession with history which disabled action in the present. In making his case, Nietzsche distinguishes between three uses of history—the antiquarian, the monumental, and the critical. While antiquarian history seeks to preserve the past and monumental history wishes to emulate it, critical history aims to liberate the present from its claims. These three uses of history are identified with three attitudes—the historical, the suprahistorical, and the unhistorical respectively. For Nietzsche, the historical attitude has become a historical sickness (the interminable rumination of the past) and requires the antidotes of the suprahistorical (an orientation towards the eternally valid examples of the past) and the unhistorical (a deliberate forgetting of the past in the interests of the present) in order to maintain what he calls the 'hygiene of life'. Nietzsche in the early 1870s was, in a sense, advocating a new historicism to replace the old, and it is this new historicism which was later to become the genealogy of morals, with its renewed commitment to the themes of forgetting and memory and the physiological imagery of health and sickness.

If the similarities and differences between the early and late work are instructive, it is also important to grasp the relationship between the *Genealogy* and the work which immediately precedes it—*Beyond Good and Evil* (1886). In his subtitle Nietzsche explicitly presents the *Genealogy* as a companion piece to *Beyond Good and Evil*. The *Genealogy* might, in fact, be seen as an extended development of some of the paragraphs of *Beyond Good and Evil*—Nietzsche regards it as part of the function of the First Essay to explain the title of his previous book. But the *Genealogy* is not derived exclusively from the preoccupations of *Beyond Good and Evil*—cross-references to other works abound, notably in the Preface, which outlines the derivation of some of the text's key ideas (Preface §4).

The Preface also proposes the Third Essay as a guide to reading Nietzsche's writings as a whole, as an example of how to decipher his more elliptic or aphoristic texts (Preface §8). The whole of the Third Essay stands as an interpretation of its epigraph and perhaps also as an explication of the paradox identified in its opening paragraph. Further, the Preface defines the minimum conditions for a successful reading—first, a thorough acquaintance with its author's previous writings; and second, a capacity for rumination. However, given the fact that the argument of the *Genealogy* is self-contained enough to stand on its own, all the first-time reader really requires is the ability to ponder and digest its ideas at length.

Backgrounds: 'English Psychology', Philology, Genealogy

The *Genealogy* refers not only to Nietzsche's earlier books but also implies a fairly wide range of work by other writers in a number of fields. In the interests of his critique of Judaeo-Christian ethics, Nietzsche both appeals to and dismisses the authority of a variety of intellectual disciplines. From the outset, Nietzsche refers frequently to the 'English psychologists' (Preface §4, I §§2–3). This operates as a general pejorative term for a range of developments in thought identified with Victorian England—the Utilitarian philosophy of Bentham and Mill, the associationist psychology of Mill and Alexander Bain, Darwin's theory of evolution and its application to sociology as Social Darwinism by figures such as Herbert Spencer. In Germany these ideas are associated with the work of Nietzsche's erstwhile friend Paul Rée. Nietzsche vigorously contests the Darwinian assumptions that natural selection is regulated by the ability to adapt successfully (the survival of the fittest) and that the present use of an organ somehow explains the whole course of its development (II §12). He also attacks the psychological explanation of cultural practices in terms of their habitual usefulness (I §§2–3). For Nietzsche, both explanations ignore the role of the will to power in the constitution of cultural phenomena—as a result of the conflict it engenders, the meanings and uses of any object or practice are never definitively fixed but remain subject to redefinition within an ongoing struggle over values.

A second field of enquiry which provides an implicit background to Nietzsche's work is that of comparative philology and anthropology—the study of other languages and cultures. Nietzsche's etymological quest for the original shared root which will explain the common derivation of ethical terms from a number of different languages is unthinkable without the similar procedures adopted by nineteenth-century philologists such as Franz Bopp in their attempts to reconstruct the lost language of the Indo-Europeans. Similarly, the ethnographic material he marshals to support his argument for the universal primacy of aristocratic ethics is drawn from a wide variety of cultures, ranging from the Celtic to the Chinese, and implies an acquaintance with contemporary anthropological and historical studies by figures such as his long-standing friend Paul Deussen. One culture does, however, take precedence in Nietzsche's critique of Judaeo-Christian ethics—the Greco-Roman tradition, with which he was familiar as a result of his professional activity as a classicist. From his earliest work on, Nietzsche represents Greek culture as a life-affirming alternative to the ascetic tradition of Judaism and Christianity, an example of a society in which suffering does not pose a problem, and the function of religion is to excuse rather than to induce guilt. In this, he forms part of a distinguished German tradition of dissident Hellenism, including the poets Hölderlin and Heine, which used its knowledge of ancient civilizations to criticize contemporary German culture rather than to support the current social order. In Nietzsche's specific case, his counter-cultural representation of the Greeks as ruthless hedonists constitutes a refusal to surrender the classical tradition to either a sanitizing liberal humanism or a self-aggrandizing Wilhelmine imperialism in search of historical precedents.

The third area of enquiry which provides a context for Nietzsche's work is that of genealogy itself. In turning to genealogical investigation in the 1880s, Nietzsche was far from alone. Darwin's work on the development of species had generated widespread interest in the reconstruction of genealogical relations, and as a result the model of the family tree or, in anthropological terms, kinship structure came to underpin a wide variety of scientific and fictional texts of the period. As the nineteenth century drew to a close, the model of genealogy became closely associated with that of pathology or the diagnosis and identification of disease. An increasing number of social critics began to react to the poverty, disease, and crime of modern industrial society by rhetorically transforming the sickness induced by poor living and working conditions from a literal effect of social deprivation into a metaphorical cause of social decay. Cultural critics had recourse to the same metaphor when confronting bohemian experimentation with new life-styles and gender roles. So a wide range of political, cultural, and ethical questions came increasingly to be discussed in the apparently neutral and scientifically persuasive language of medicine and health, as critics of contemporary decadence developed a technique of symptomatic reading whereby any phenomenon might be interpreted as a symptom of some underlying sickness. And, in the view of many commentators, *fin-de-siècle* society was intrinsically sick, diseased, pathological—its members were degenerating, as the privileged became hopelessly weak and effete and the disadvantaged regressed down the evolutionary scale into animality. In many ways the projected future of H. G. Wells's *The Time Machine* (1895) sums up this double anxiety, with its depiction of a pastoral society of helpless, childlike adults (the Eloi) preyed upon by monstrous subterranean workers (the Morlocks).

The widespread preoccupation with supposed degeneracy led to a number of attempts to trace the inheritance of assumed disease through blood-lines or family trees—hence, for example, works such as Max Nordau's *Degeneracy* (1893), Zola's *Rougon-*

Macquart cycle of novels (1871–93), or Thomas Mann's *Buddenbrooks* (1901). Nietzsche's genealogy is, like these texts, an exercise in cultural pathology, an attempt to account for the supposed decay of contemporary society in the biological or physiological terms of sickness and health, but his approach differs in certain significant respects. First, Nietzsche locates decadence not in deviation from respectable social convention but in conformity to it—in so doing he runs against the grain of most contemporary literature on the subject. Secondly, Nietzsche's use of the family tree or kinship model is for the most part looser than that of his contemporaries. The naturalist novel typically narrates its family romance as a gradual process of disintegration across several generations, as a result of inherited weakness or disease. Its notion of genealogy is fairly literal and fatalistic—the inevitable transmission of pathology through the blood. Nietzsche's genealogy, in contrast, is much less literal and more optimistically interventionist. Genealogy is envisaged here as the historical study of the multiple intersecting forces which produce the meaning of a given phenomenon or practice. So the study of these forces reconstructs a metaphorical rather than a literal kinship network. Furthermore, the interplay of forces described is an ongoing struggle whose outcome is yet to be determined, and so allows for the possibility of intervention.

As an approach to history, Nietzsche's notion and practice of genealogy challenges the accepted methodologies of his day. Just as he had done some years earlier in *On the Use and Disadvantage...*, Nietzsche rejects the progressive notion of history as a necessary, rule-governed development which finds its fulfilment either in the present or in some deferred future. In this respect he dissents both from the Enlightenment view of history as progress and from the deterministic theory of historical development associated with Hegel. Furthermore, Nietzsche also rejects the more contemporary view, associated with Leopold Ranke, of history as a given object of neutral scientific description. While the genealogies to be found in naturalist literature combine elements of the determinist (Hegelian) and descriptive (Rankean) approaches offered by the historiography of the day, Nietzsche's cultural critique is of a markedly different kind. In contrast to the naturalist novel, which works inexorably inwards from its documentary record of environmental factors towards the genetically programmed moment of disaster which destroys the family, Nietzsche's genealogy works outwards from the present disastrous state of humanity as he sees it towards an understanding of the many interacting factors which have produced this state. This understanding then furnishes the basis for intervention in the present struggle over values.

In certain important respects, Nietzsche's practice of genealogy is not only diagnostic and interventionist but also self-reflexive. As well as providing a genealogy of morals, Nietzsche presents a genealogy of his own ideas and approach, an outline of what he considers to have been the most important contributions to the field and the most significant influences on his own view of the problem. This outline of intellectual kinship (and lack of it) takes the form of numerous cross-references both to works which anticipate his present concerns and also to works which his own ideas refute. The result is a kind of intellectual family tree including more or less sympathetic 'relatives' such as Schopenhauer, Wagner, Darwin, and Paul Rée. Genealogy shades over into bibliography here, to constitute a form of autobiography which Nietzsche was to develop more explicitly in *Ecce Homo* (1888/1908) with a discussion of actual as well as intellectual kinship.

As the central explanatory model of the text, genealogy is represented in a variety of ways. Although Nietzsche's overall sense of genealogy is not literal, the conventional sense of genealogy as blood-line surfaces at points in his recourse to metaphors of breeding to describe the development of human memory (II §1). But the most frequently recurring image for the genealogical development of phenomena is not that of livestock breeding but that of the growth of a (family) tree—genealogy is at times the record of a search for the roots of a cultural phenomenon, at others the pursuit of its multiple ramifications, the observation of changes in the course of its development, the insistence upon the careful distinctions to be made between root and branch, between a tree and its fruit (I §7, II §2). In a sense, these multiple meanings and images of genealogy are inevitable. Nietzsche may appear to use the term 'genealogy' in a relatively unproblematic way to describe the historical study of the ramifications which lead outwards from concepts in which a number of meanings intersect, but, as the text reveals in its references and imagery, the notion of genealogy is in its own right a complex and ramified concept.

The Critique of Ethics

The complex and ramified set of concepts which forms the principal subject of the *Genealogy* is, however, the system of morality which in Nietzsche's view governed late nineteenth-century Europe. The *Genealogy*'s critique of Christian and liberal humanist values takes the form of a counter-narrative to the Enlightenment view of historical development as one of progress and emancipation. For Nietzsche, the dominant values controlling the morality of late nineteenth-century Europe—equality, justice, and compassion—are not the timeless absolutes they purport to be but the outcome of a violent struggle between two opposed systems of value—what he calls the aristocratic morality and the slave morality. For Nietzsche, the moralities in question are not values based in objective truths but reflections of the concrete interests of those who subscribe to them. The aristocratic morality is historically the earlier of the two systems and is characterized by an ethic of active and ruthless self-affirmation, whereas the slave morality is the reactive and resentful response of the weak to their domination by the self-affirming strong. In Nietzschean terms, the former is driven by a will to power which seeks always to expend its available energy, even to the point of death, while the latter is motivated by *ressentiment* and is obsessed with conservation and self-preservation. So the central opposition between aristocratic and slave moralities is accompanied throughout by the opposition between their respective informing principles of an active and healthy will to power, forever seeking to increase its power in physical terms, and a reactive and sickly *ressentiment*, desperately seeking to preserve, through devious intellectual means whatever power it has attained to. Nietzsche holds that the two moralities and their accompanying principles are incommensurable, separated by what he calls the 'pathos of distance'. However, by virtue of the stealth and cunning fostered by *ressentiment*, the slave morality has in the course of history managed to undermine the hegemony of the aristocratic morality and stage what Nietzsche calls the slave revolt in morals. In the process, the values of *ressentiment*, founded upon a violent repression of instinct, have come to dominate Western culture and have established themselves as the absolute foundation of ethics. Such for Nietzsche is the legacy bequeathed by the Judaic and Christian traditions to modern secular liberalism and socialism. And for Nietzsche it is a hopelessly destructive and demoralizing legacy—in his view, the hegemony of slave morality represents a threat to the development of humanity in so far as its egalitarian values promote weakness and mediocrity at the expense of vitality and dynamism, substituting the inevitable goal of gradual universal progress for the random possibility of outstanding individual achievement. This analysis of the slave revolt in morals is based upon that sketched out in *Beyond Good and Evil*, §195. In the *Genealogy*, it is developed into an anthropological and historical narrative extended across three essays.

The First Essay sets out to investigate the origin of moral values through an etymological quest for the root meanings of ethical terms. The argument from etymology seeks to establish the former primacy of aristocratic ethics. For Nietzsche, all ethical terms are derived from terms denoting social rank, which are in turn assumed to designate essential qualities. The original aristocratic morality operated on the basis of a distinction between 'good' (its own health, strength, and will) and 'bad' (the sickness, weakness, and *ressentiment* of the lower classes). The slave revolt in morals succeeded in reversing this schema, redesignating the weak as 'good' and the strong as 'evil', thereby producing the current moral orthodoxy and effacing its original predecessor. Nietzsche is careful to point out how this reversal came about in part through the activities of a priestly caste within the aristocracy itself. For Nietzsche, the struggle between the opposing value systems is not definitively over—it has been fought out again and again across the generations and has even been internalized in the psychology of the best of his contemporaries.

The Second Essay opens with an account of the history of memory and the capacity to promise. While the ability to remember is what distinguishes humanity from the animals, the capacity to promise is for Nietzsche what distinguishes the aristocrat from the slave. The self-discipline necessary to keep a promise is the product of an active aristocratic will. But if memory allows the keeping of promises, it also permits a less healthy dwelling on the past. The Second Essay continues with a history of 'bad conscience', 'guilt', and an investigation into the origin and purpose of punishment. 'Bad conscience' is identified as the result of the repression of the active instincts, forcing these to turn in upon the self. 'Guilt' for Nietzsche is etymologically derived from 'debt', and originates in the economic relationship between creditor and debtor. Debtors who default on their repayments are subjected to harsh physical punishment, intended both to gratify the creditor and to inculcate a greater sense of responsibility in the defaulter. Such punishments include branding and amputation, practices which produce the depths of the soul (feelings of remorse and revenge) by inscribing and defacing the surface of the body. So all civilization for Nietzsche is a product of economically sanctioned violence. The contract between creditor and debtor, regulated by the threat of ruthless force, forms the anthropological matrix for the development of justice, religion, and the state. These institutions do not derive from consensual agreement between equal parties, as a theorist such as Rousseau would have it, but are originally imposed from above or without, thereby engendering an ineradicable sense of indebtedness. In terms of the origin of 'bad conscience' and 'guilt', the history of human culture is not one of progress towards greater equality and compassion but a history of cruelty, both self-inflicted and socially imposed.

The Third Essay presents itself as an exercise in interpretation, designed in the first place to explain its own epigraph—'Unconcerned, contemptuous, violent—this is how wisdom would have us be: she is a woman, she only ever loves a warrior.' It should be noted, however, that if the essay does explain how wisdom may be attained through violence and domination, it does so obliquely. The more explicit task which the Third Essay sets itself is that of accounting for the paradox that the will prefers to will nothingness rather than not will. The will in question here is, of course, will to power, the force which, in Nietzsche's view, informs and drives all human activity and as such comes to be identified with life itself. The paradox is resolved through an investigation into the meaning of what Nietzsche calls the ascetic ideal, the ideal of self-abnegation and self-castigation. Since the self-inflicted cruelty of the ascetic ideal is apparently a thoroughly self-destructive phenomenon—in Nietzsche's terms, a manifestation of life opposed to life—it represents in itself a further paradox requiring explanation. The figure through whom the ascetic ideal becomes hegemonic is the ascetic priest introduced in the First Essay. His main function is to redirect the *ressentiment* of the weak back against themselves, thus protecting the strong from any acts of revenge. The priest convinces the weak that they are responsible for their own suffering (whose initial causes are, for Nietzsche, purely physiological) and persuades them to take refuge in the ascetic ideal. The ultimate purpose of the ascetic ideal is to justify the suffering of the weak and to reconcile them to life—it thus affirms life in spite of itself, since it is the most characteristic expression of the will to power of the weak. And so it becomes clear how the will prefers to will nothing (the ascetic ideal) rather than not will, since regardless of its object it thereby expresses itself as will to power. In the process of explaining this paradox the essay also explains its epigraph—wisdom is attainable through violence because the will to truth of the ascetic ideal creates fictional truths (the values of slave morality) whose violent distortion of history can only be opposed by a violent counter-interpretation of the kind practised by Nietzsche.

In the course of this extended argument, the 'absolute values' of slave morality which Nietzsche is attacking are discredited in three main ways—slave morality is in turn historicized, demystified, and pathologized. First, its supposedly timeless values are revealed as the contingent products of historical struggle. Secondly, its supposedly disinterested values are shown to derive from a material basis in debt and credit. Thirdly, its supposedly transcendent values are traced back to bodily dysfunction. The primary methodological resources for this critique are etymology, economic anthropology, and physiology respectively. On one level, the genealogy of morals is a quest for the original meanings of ethical terms effaced by the slave revolt in morals. On another, it is the search for the ruthless creditor–debtor relations which underlie the fictions of free and equal citizens entering into a social contract. On another level again, it is a symptomatic reading of liberal ethics and the psychology of guilt and compassion as the effects of some physiological disorder.

This triple project is fraught with complications and paradoxes. In the first place, if the argument from etymology seeks some putative origin for ethical terms, Nietzsche elsewhere argues that the genealogical history of any practice renders origins strictly irretrievable, since each new meaning or function effaces the last (II §§6, 13). He also warns about the danger of being misled into philosophical error by the arbitrary structures of language (I §13). Secondly, there is the problem that indebtedness ultimately presupposes some kind of contract and assumes the possibility of some kind of repayment or equivalent settlement between the parties involved (II §14). Finally, Nietzsche argues at various points that the notion of the body is relative and mutable, dependent on cultural definitions to give it form, in which case it cannot explain anything but is itself in need of explanation (II §§12, 16).

There is a similar problem with the central historical thesis of the book, that of the slave revolt in morals which usurps the hegemony of aristocratic morality. As the argument progresses, it becomes increasingly clear that aristocratic morality is not defeated from without but from within, that it allows itself to be usurped. According to Nietzsche, the masters' capacity for self-discipline gradually leads to the creation of a priest caste which begins to inculcate guilt and self-loathing in the strong (II §§17, 18). The active instincts are thus in a sense the agents of their own cultural repression. Further, the domination of the weak by the strong creates the conditions for their conversion to the ascetic ideal (II §17). So aristocratic morality collaborates with the *ressentiment* it despises, just as slave morality is driven by the will to power it repudiates (II §18, III §§9, 13). This is the dual paradox which renders problematic the initial premiss of Nietzsche's argument—the irreducible pathos of distance between aristocratic and slave moralities. In fact, as Nietzsche demonstrates, at any moment each morality is capable of assuming the form of the other.

In part, this confusion of will to power with *ressentiment* explains Nietzsche's ambivalence towards the achievements of slave morality. For Nietzsche, humanity under the influence of the ascetic ideal has become not just a sick animal but also an interesting animal (I §7). Self-denial and self-punishment have produced an inner life where none existed before (II §16), and have developed and enhanced new human capacities such as responsibility and the ability to change perspective (III §12). Furthermore, beyond a certain point it becomes impossible to distinguish between the effects of *ressentiment* and will to power—the development of the capacity to remember is at one moment the product of aristocratic self-discipline (II §1) and at another of the conditioning of the weak through physical punishment (II §3); the organization of the masses is variously the work of the aristocrat who founds the state (II §17) and of the ascetic priest who fosters the herd instinct (III §15). As Nietzsche says, it is in fact the same active force which both builds states and instils bad conscience (II §18). Unfortunately, the distinction he proposes between a will exercised on others and a will exercised on the self becomes increasingly difficult to maintain.

Nietzsche's lingering fascination with what he ostensibly repudiates may derive in part from his view that the conflict between aristocratic and slave moralities is no longer a social struggle but has been internalized as a psychological conflict. In that sense, the genealogy of his own psyche must include the interplay of will to power and *ressentiment*—a position he seems to adopt later in *Ecce Homo* when he describes his own work as both a symptom of decadence and the symbol of a new beginning ('Why I Am So Wise', §1). Such ambiguities, however revealing psychologically, complicate the search for an uncompromised truth on which to base a critique of values.

Science and Art, Truth and Interpretation

The relationships between science, art, truth, and interpretation are central to an understanding of the *Genealogy*. In fact, much of the latter part of the book is devoted to them. When approaching Nietzsche's comments on science, it is important in the first place to remember that the term is ambiguous. As a result of the Continental tendency to divide academic disciplines into natural and human sciences, 'science' need not refer exclusively to physics, chemistry, biology, and their offshoots. So when Nietzsche mentions science, he may be referring either to the natural sciences or, as is frequently the case, to the application of scientific approaches in the humanities, and particularly in history. Nietzsche associates these approaches with the work of historians such as Leopold Ranke and Ernest Renan, who sought to reconstruct historical events as they had happened on the basis of rigorous factual research and verifiable sources.

If Nietzsche's use of the term 'science' is ambiguous, so is his attitude to it. As we have seen, his critique of ethics depends in large part on a scientific methodology (the resources of etymology, economic anthropology, and physiology), yet much of the *Genealogy* undertakes a radical critique of the presuppositions of science. In brief, Nietzsche's critique of science runs as follows. Science may appear to oppose and demystify the superstition of religion and its life-denying ascetic ideal, but this is merely a superficial opposition. For Nietzsche, science is, in fact, the ultimate form of the ascetic ideal, the ascetic ideal reduced to its essence as will to truth. For science is what remains once the Judaeo-Christian tradition turns its own ethical standards against itself, once the quest for truth initially cultivated by religion discredits the authenticity of biblical and theological accounts of human history. Religion may have lost its persuasiveness, but its essential commitment to truth survives and goes from strength to strength in the form of its scientific antagonist.

In fact, the will to truth is, for Nietzsche, the ultimate expression of the slave morality. So long as it maintains its claim to objectivity, science can never challenge the hegemony of *ressentiment*. Only an activity which has dispensed with truth once and for all can conceivably do so. In these terms, the only escape from the ascetic ideal is through art. Art has no pretensions to truth—its lies declare themselves as such. Unlike the fictions of religion, morality, and science, the fictions of art do not seek to pass themselves off as truths, but present themselves as what they are (III §25).

This rejection of truth as just another form of the insidious and life-denying ascetic ideal raises the fundamental question of the status of Nietzsche's own argument. The *Genealogy* appears to present itself initially as a demystification of current assumptions about Christian and liberal values, a demystification implicitly founded upon the revelation of the *true* origins of moral concepts. But if Nietzsche dismisses truth as yet another value in need of demystification, upon what basis does he ground his own argument? His critique of truth would seem to discredit the genealogical project as a quest for truth. Further, how is the dismissal of truth itself grounded? Any dismissal of truth paradoxically presupposes its own truthfulness. Does such a dismissal then cancel itself out by denying its own truth-value even as it asserts it? Not even Nietzsche's appeal to the essentially perspectival nature of truth can arrest this paradoxical spiral. To declare that all truths are nothing more than interested and partial perspectives on events which are neutral in themselves assumes that the theory of perspectivism itself is true. So, in its own terms, the perspectivist argument leaves itself open to dismissal as merely another groundless perspective. The infinite regress occasioned by this interrogation of the value of truth is a fundamental feature of Nietzsche's style of argument, its ultimate tendency to call itself into question.

This rejection of science in favour of art, of truth in favour of fiction, is borne out in Nietzsche's style of writing. As has often been noted by commentators, his style is highly metaphorical, drawing on a wide range of figurative language to illustrate his argument—the recurring images of plants and trees slip into those of predatory and caged animals, sickness and health, strength and weakness, and back again. His general (highly questionable) strategy is to use images of the natural world to describe cultural phenomena, thereby suggesting that social developments may somehow be evaluated in terms of their naturalness or lack of it. But the slippage between different fields of imagery obscures this evaluation, and it becomes increasingly difficult to distinguish between the fruit of sovereignty and the weed of *ressentiment*, the self-control of a predator and the timidity of a tame domestic animal. It also becomes increasingly difficult for the reader to differentiate between images and concepts, particularly with regard to the premisses of the argument, such as the pathos of distance assumed to separate the aristocratic from the slave moralities. Is this irreducible distance conceptually grounded in social difference, as the names of the two moralities suggest, or in racial difference (the antagonists are sometimes described as members of different races), in gender difference (the aristocrat is typically masculine, the slave feminine), in differences of physical type (the aristocrat is strong and healthy, the slave weak and sickly), in evolutionary decay (the aristocrat is a healthy primitive, the slave over-refined to the point of degeneracy)? Each of these apparently conceptual oppositions seems at times to operate as a metaphor for the others, with none ultimately providing a secure and definitive ground for the argument as a whole. As a result, Nietzsche's metaphors tend to destabilize rather than support his argument.

This use of metaphor may help to account for Nietzsche's paradoxical use of science to support an argument which is itself a critique of scientific presuppositions. Indeed, as we have seen, the main methodological resources he draws upon in the course of his argument are scientific—etymology, economic anthropology, and physiology. In fact, Nietzsche uses science against science, employing scientific methods and data to question the aims and motivation of science, particularly with respect to the quest for truth. So his science too is a fiction, a metaphor. This would explain how he can criticize Darwinian evolutionary theory on a conceptual level and then apparently use it as an implicit model of development (II §16). It might also explain the apparent weaknesses in the way Nietzsche deploys his methodology as a whole. His often speculative etymological connections take their lead from similarity of sound, in spite of his warnings about the 'seduction of language' (I §13). Thus, his whole argument about the centrality of creditor–debtor relations rests on the similarity between the German words for debt (*Schulden*) and guilt (*Schuld*) (II §4). His use of physiological models to explain human behaviour is likewise analogical—the physiological disorders which he diagnoses operate as materialist metaphors for the working of the psyche, so that, for example, problems in coming to terms with a particular experience may be described as a form of indigestion (II §1). In a sense, then, in Nietzsche's hands science becomes metaphorical, is enlisted in the service of art, of fiction rather than truth. His primary methodological resource turns out not to be etymology, economic anthropology, or physiology but analogy.

What then is the purpose of Nietzsche's scientific fiction? In his reliance on metaphors and etymological puns like *Schulden/Schuld*, Nietzsche is a practitioner as well as a critic of the 'seduction of language'. In fact, his style is not just metaphorical but also highly rhetorical—with its emphatic punctuation and italics, the text almost seems scored for oral delivery. Traditionally, rhetoric is the art of persuasion—it has no necessary relation to truth. And in fact, Nietzsche seems to deploy his stylistic resources not to establish truths but in an effort to persuade and provoke his readers. This double function is important—he is not seeking so much to convince a passive reader as to antagonize a potentially active one. For Nietzsche, one local manifestation of will to power seeks not solely to dominate another but to elicit some kind of response from it, in the interests of maximizing the overall expenditure of power. In these terms, the primary purpose of the argument-as-fiction is to provoke a reaction, to generate a polemic. As a polemical text, the *Genealogy* aims to incite the kind of conflict over values which it appears to document.

For it is not at all certain that Nietzsche's genealogy does actually document historical conflict in any conventional sense. This uncertainty results in part from the fact that the text advances two competing models of interpretation. On the one hand, Nietzsche emphasizes the need for patient textual study and a scrupulous approach to historical evidence (Preface §7).

This model is implicitly picked up throughout the argument in a series of images which refer to a wide range of cultural practices in terms of reading and writing, legibility and textuality. On the other hand, Nietzsche also stresses the essentially violent nature of any interpretation, its necessarily interested and partial character (III §24). The way in which the Third Essay is presented as an interpretation of its epigraph ('wisdom [...] is a woman, she only ever loves a warrior') stresses in gendered terms the violent and dominating nature of the will to knowledge. The conflict between these competing models of interpretation—fidelity to the text versus forceful imposition of meaning—poses the question of whether the task of genealogical investigation is to uncover and document the violence of past interpretations or whether it is itself another act of interpretative violence. Does genealogy represent an attempt to expose an implicitly interested deformation of the past or is this attempt itself just another deformation of the past in line with different and more explicit interests? This returns us to the insoluble paradoxes raised by Nietzsche's relationship to truth—the *Genealogy* appears to offer an alternative historical account of the development of ethical values, but it also calls the very possibility of such an account into question. If objective truth is a violently imposed fiction, then so is any interpretation founded upon it. But to assert that objective truth is a fiction is to make a statement of objective truth, which thereby denounces itself as a fiction. Once again the text opens up the dizzying perspective of infinite regress. In the process, it confronts the reader with a dilemma and the necessity of making some sort of choice both about the sets of values it brings into conflict and the kinds of interpretation which are appropriate to them.

After the Genealogy

The *Genealogy* has proved to be one of Nietzsche's most provocative and influential works, both in content and form of argument. Ironically, in view of Nietzsche's attempt to replace psychology with physiology, many of his insights into the operation of repression and sublimation anticipate concepts later developed by Freud. The theory of cultural development outlined in *Civilization and its Discontents* (1930) clearly resembles that outlined by Nietzsche in certain important respects, while the ambiguities of the conflict between Eros and Thanatos delineated in *Beyond the Pleasure Principle* (1920) recall the struggle between will to power and *ressentiment*. The *Genealogy* was also to provide literary inspiration for subsequent writers. Kafka's short story 'In the Penal Colony' (1919), in which criminals are executed by having an illegible sentence written into their flesh by a torture machine, is often regarded as a development of the sections of the Second Essay which deal with the origin of conscience and the internalization of the law.

In the 1930s and 1940s, the appropriation of Nietzsche by the National Socialist movement largely ignored the subtleties of argument in the *Genealogy* in favour of a vulgar reading of the recurring figure of the 'blond beast' (I §11, II §17) as an unproblematic representative of the Aryan master-race driven by an irresistible will to power. Such a reading had been prepared by the tendentious interpretation and editing of Nietzsche's work by his sister Elisabeth, a convinced anti-Semite. But the Nazi version ignored both the specificity of Nietzsche's imagery and its context. In the first place, the image of the blond beast refers not to any literal ideal of racial purity but to the metaphorical opposition between the predatory animal of aristocratic morality and the domesticated or caged animal of slave morality. Secondly, Nietzsche clearly holds that the aristocratic and slave moralities are not the monopoly of particular ethnic groups but are to be found across a wide range of very different cultures and societies. Nietzsche was by no means free from the racial prejudices of his age, as his remarks on African susceptibility to pain demonstrate (II §7), but he was not an anti-Semite. In fact, he vehemently opposed organized anti-Semitism, which he regarded as a product of vulgar *ressentiment* (II §11, III §§14, 26). His derogatory remarks on the subject of Judaism (I §§7, 8) are of a piece with his contempt for Christianity and socialism (I §9). Judaism, like a number of other subsequent political and religious movements, is for Nietzsche simply a successful manifestation of the slave morality, and as a result elicits both scathing criticism and a kind of grudging admiration. It is this ambiguity which makes selective quotation for racist ends possible, but which also means that any attentive reading cannot fail to appreciate the distortion necessary to make Nietzsche into an apologist for genocide.

In spite of its distortions, the Nazi appropriation exerted a considerable influence on post-war Nietzsche studies. By the late 1950s, however, thanks to the work of commentators such as Walter Kaufmann, Nietzsche had been rehabilitated as a respectable philosopher. Kaufmann re-canonized Nietzsche in part by relating his work to that of other important German thinkers such as Freud and Hegel, translating terminological into conceptual similarities. For Kaufmann, Nietzsche's theory of the will to power was a kind of 'dialectical monism'—since will to power was envisaged as the single vital force informing all life, it represented a form of monism, but since it could only manifest itself by constantly opposing itself, constantly dividing against itself to generate new conflicts, it appeared in split form in a series of dialectical clashes.

Partly because of its appropriation by National Socialism, the Marxist tradition has always viewed Nietzsche's critique of ethics with ambivalence. On the one hand, his theory of an underlying will to power is seen to demystify both the self-serving and self-destructive aspects of bourgeois morality and culture. As a result, Nietzsche figures quite strongly in the work of theorists such as Theodor Adorno, Walter Benjamin, and Max Horkheimer. Adorno and Horkheimer's *Dialectic of Enlightenment* (1944), with its critique of rationalist thought as a new obscurantism and its identification of culture as the product of self-sacrifice, clearly echoes Nietzschean themes, as does Benjamin's insistence, in his *Theses on the Philosophy of History* (1940), on the status of culture as the document of barbarism. On the other hand, Nietzsche's *fin-de-siècle* dismissal of an ethics of compassion in the name of will to power may also be viewed as an oblique apologia for the ruthlessness of capitalism in its most rapacious phase of imperialist expansion. Such is the response outlined by Georg Lukács in *The Destruction of Reason* (1954). The majority of subsequent Marxist commentators have tended to occupy one of these two positions, while a few have attempted to reconcile them. Meanwhile, commentators from outside the Marxist tradition have sought to establish structural links between the thought of Nietzsche and Marx.

In the 1960s Nietzsche became widely associated with Marx and Freud as a practitioner of what the philosopher Paul Ricoeur called the hermeneutics of suspicion—a style of interpretation which uncovers latent meanings through a suspicious reading of an untrustworthy surface (for Nietzsche, this took the form of the discovery of the operation of will to power in supposedly disinterested values; for Marx, the exposure of the economic forces which determine apparently autonomous cultural activities; for Freud, the revelation of the unconscious desires concealed beneath the surface of dreams). The view of Nietzsche as symptomatologist was challenged by Michel Foucault and Susan Sontag amongst others, who both saw in his work a suspicion of depth rather than of surface, a reading of depth as the effect of an inscribed surface (in line with Nietzsche's interpretation of conscience as the product of branding in the Second Essay).

In a number of essays on historiography, Foucault also elaborated on a theoretical level the Nietzschean project of genealogical study, before proceeding to analyse in more detail the social functions of cruelty and punishment in *Discipline and Punish* (1975) and the inescapable ramifications of power in the first volume of his *History of Sexuality* (1976). In philosophy, Gilles Deleuze based his influential explication of Nietzsche's work as a whole on his account of the two moralities, stressing the difference between active and reactive forces (*Nietzsche and Philosophy*, 1962). Nietzsche also provided a frequent point of reference for another influential French philosopher, Jacques Derrida, who saw in his work an anticipation of the theory and practice of deconstruction. The argument of the *Genealogy*, for example, might be said to deconstruct itself as it unfolds, in so far as it gradually undoes the assumptions and distinctions from which it proceeds. Overall, as a result of its importance within French philosophical debate in the 1960s and 1970s, the *Genealogy* has attained the status of a central text in the history of interpretation.

More recent interest in Nietzsche has tended to focus on questions relating to gender and the body. The debate turns in the first instance on the question of whether Nietzsche has anything to offer contemporary feminism. Nietzsche's work as a whole is notorious for its explicit misogyny, and the *Genealogy* is no exception. The terms of the argument are clearly gendered throughout—will to power, aristocratic morality, health are all masculine, while *ressentiment*, slave morality, and sickness are all either feminine or feminized. The difference between will to power and *ressentiment* is figured as one of castration (III §§12, 26). In line with the well-known opening words of *Beyond Good and Evil*—'Assuming that truth is a woman...'—truth and wisdom are represented as women, fawning but treacherous ideals desiring domination by a male seeker after knowledge (Epigraph to the Third Essay, III §24). Political feminism is denounced as a life-denying form of the ascetic ideal (III §§19, 27). There is one significant qualification to this association of the feminine with the negative, and as a traditional Romantic topos it is far from radical—male creativity is described in terms of pregnancy and gestation (II §19, III §8). Otherwise, the issue of Nietzsche's usefulness has to be decided on the basis of whether his blurring of the distinction between will to power and *ressentiment* extends to the gendered categories associated with them, whether the positions of domination and submission traditionally identified as masculine and feminine are thereby loosened or destabilized. Central to this debate is the relationship between Nietzsche's figure of truth as woman and his denial of the existence of truth—does this double move free women from fixed and essentialist definitions of identity, or simply reinforce already entrenched stereotypes about feminine fickleness and unreliability? Some commentators maintain that the former is the case, while others see in Nietzsche's work nothing more than another example of patriarchal prejudice and a traditional recuperation of those aspects of femininity (such as biological reproduction in its literal and metaphorical forms) useful to continued male supremacy.

The status of the body is a related issue, and in some ways Nietzsche's argument outlines the main positions taken in recent discussions. On the one hand, his recourse to symptomatic readings of cultural phenomena in physiological terms seems to assume that the body may function unproblematically as ground of knowledge or basis for critique (Note to the First Essay). On the other hand, he also seems to suggest that the body is a cultural construct which cannot be isolated from the forces which give it its contingent meanings, and is thus implicitly incapable of functioning as a ground (II §§12, 16). Located between these positions is a third view of the body as a passive surface for the inscription of cultural meanings, both assumed to exist in its own right prior to acculturation yet subject to redefinition by cultural forces. All three positions are reproduced within current discussions of the status of the body within feminism, where a desire to retain some notion of the specificity of sexual difference grounded in the body encounters a commitment to the cultural construction of gender roles. However divergent these apparent alternatives may seem, they are coming increasingly to be regarded as complementary rather than incompatible. Within the context of a patriarchal system which operates in terms of contradictory definitions of the feminine (women may be condemned for being both unfathomable and shallow, for having both too much essence and too little), the flexibility of a dual response which is strategically sensitive to context offers certain advantages over a single dogmatic position—it becomes possible to meet the accusation of unfathomability with an analysis of the superficiality of the mysterious and enigmatic essence attributed to woman, and to counter the accusation of shallowness with an analysis of the depth of superficiality (as essence) which such an accusation paradoxically presupposes. This is perhaps the most notable part of Nietzsche's current legacy—a distrust of fixed positions which permits a flexible and strategic approach to argument—and it is an approach which is to be found in any number of fields of study where notions of identity and essence are at issue.

Conclusion

On the Genealogy of Morals, then, is a text which engages with important issues of its day but retains a relevance to the concerns of the present. Many of the values it criticizes are still currently held more or less without question, and recent philosophical critiques of complacent versions of liberal humanism have taken inspiration from Nietzsche. Equally, many of the implications of his methodological choices resonate within current debates over essentialism in gender and post-colonial studies. In these respects, the *Genealogy* has retained the capacity to reveal that what passes for depth is often little more than skin deep. Furthermore, the *Genealogy* is a text which raises fundamental questions about practices of reading and interpretation and then proceeds to implicate itself in these questions—making claims it appears to disavow, challenging its own foundations, revealing the superficiality of its own depths. In this it anticipates many recent developments in textual studies and literary criticism. In both content and form, then, both as a book about the history of ethics and as a book about interpretation, it is a text which continues to make demands on its readers' capacity for rumination, but which demands to be read none the less.

NOTE ON THE TRANSLATION

The two English translations of *On the Genealogy of Morals* most readily available in paperback are American imprints: the version co-authored by Walter Kaufmann and R. J. Hollingdale (Vintage) and that by Francis Golffing (Doubleday). Golffing's is quite a free version, and most readers are more familiar with the Kaufmann and Hollingdale translation. Although a very fine version in many respects, the latter has a tendency, in line with Kaufmann's critical readings, to assimilate Nietzsche's ideas and terminology to those of Hegel and Freud. I have sought to distinguish more clearly between what seem to me to be very different projects, using notes where clarification or qualification seemed appropriate. In general, the notes are intended to give some sense of the contemporary intellectual context in which Nietzsche wrote and of how his method and arguments relate to this. For a good annotated edition of the German text, readers should refer to Peter Pütz's Goldmann Klassiker volume (1983). The original text for this translation is taken from the sparsely annotated Colli–Montinari edition of Nietzsche's complete works (Berlin: De Gruyter, 1967).

Within the text itself, I have tried to make the sense as clear as possible. Particularly significant problems of translation are signalled in the notes. Arguably the single most difficult task in translating Nietzsche is, however, less that of conveying the meaning than that of rendering the style, with its constant play of rhetoric and imagery. The risk run by the translator is that of producing a flat version which reduces the verve of the original to pedantic eccentricity. How successful I have been in avoiding this is for others to judge, but I hope at least to have produced a usefully clear and readable version.

I would like to thank the following people for their advice and help as I worked on this translation: David Constantine, who kindly read and commented on early drafts; Alexander Nehamas, who offered useful guidance on notes and problems of translation; my readers and copy-editor at OUP, whose thoughtful and constructive criticism often made the work seem a co-translation; Catherine Clarke, Susie Casement, and Judith Luna, for their patience and forbearance as editors. The translation is the better for their contribution and any misjudgements or infelicities which remain are my own. Further back, thanks are also due to Angela Walls, Valerie Sorrie, Martin Lauster, Ursula and Hans-Christoph Gaupp, who all in their different ways taught me German.

SELECT BIBLIOGRAPHY

Criticism

Ahern, Daniel, *Nietzsche as Cultural Physician* (University Park, PA: Pennsylvania State University Press, 1995)

Allison, David B. (ed.), *The New Nietzsche: Contemporary Styles of Interpretation* (Cambridge, Mass.: MIT Press, 1985).

Burgard, Peter J. (ed.), *Nietzsche and the Feminine* (Charlottesville, Va.: University Press of Virginia, 1994).

Deleuze, Gilles, *Nietzsche and Philosophy* (London: Athlone Press, 1983).

De Man, Paul, *Allegories of Reading: Figural Language in Rousseau, Nietzsche, Rilke and Proust* (New Haven, Conn.: Yale University Press, 1979).

Hollingdale, R. J., *Nietzsche: The Man and his Philosophy* (London: Routledge & Kegan Paul, 1965).

Kaufmann, Walter, *Nietzsche: Philosopher, Psychologist, Antichrist* (Princeton, NJ: Princeton University Press, 1968).

Kofman, Sarah, *Nietzsche and Metaphor* (London: Athlone Press, 1993).

Nehamas, Alexander, *Nietzsche: Life as Literature* (Cambridge, Mass.: Harvard University Press, 1985).

Pasley, Malcolm (ed.), *Nietzsche: Imagery and Thought* (London: Methuen, 1978).

Patton, Paul (ed.), *Nietzsche, Feminism and Political Theory* (London: Routledge, 1993).

Sedgwick, Eve Kosofsky, *Epistemology of the Closet* (London: Penguin, 1994).

Schacht, Richard (ed.), *Nietzsche, Genealogy, Morality: Essays on Nietzsche's On the Genealogy of Morals* (Berkeley: University of California Press, 1994).

Stern, J. P., *Nietzsche* (London: Fontana, 1978).

Tanner, Michael, *Nietzsche* (Oxford: Oxford University Press, 1994).

White, Hayden, *Metahistory: The Historical Imagination in Nineteenth-Century Europe* (Baltimore: Johns Hopkins University Press, 1973).

Weidling, P.J., *Health, Race and German Politics between National Unification and Nazism* (Cambridge: Cambridge University Press, 1989).

Biography

Hayman, Ronald, *Nietzsche: A Critical Life* (London: Weidenfeld and Nicolson, 1980).

A CHRONOLOGY OF FRIEDRICH NIETZSCHE

1844 Birth of Friedrich Wilhelm Nietzsche in Röcken, Saxony, on 15 October, son of Karl Ludwig and Franziska Nietzsche. Nietzsche's father and both grandfathers are Protestant pastors.

1846 Birth of sister Elisabeth.

1849 Death of Karl Ludwig Nietzsche.

1850 Family moves to Naumberg.

1858–64 Nietzsche attends élite grammar school Schulpforta. Beginning of friendship with Paul Deussen.

1864 Enters Bonn University to study theology and classical philology. Reads David Strauss's *Life of Jesus*.

1865 Follows classics teacher Ritschl to Leipzig, where he drops theology and continues with studies in classical philology. Starts to read Schopenhauer.

1866 Becomes friendly with classicist Erwin Rohde.

1867 Begins military service.

1868 Injured in riding accident. Discharged from army. Meets Richard Wagner in Leipzig.

1869 On Ritschl's recommendation, appointed extraordinary professor of classical philology at Basle University. Frequents Wagner residence in Tribschen.

1870 Participates in Franco-Prussian War as volunteer medical orderly. Contracts diphtheria at the Front. Becomes friendly with theologian Franz Overbeck.

1872 Publication of *The Birth of Tragedy*. Object of polemic which compromises Nietzsche's reputation as respectable academic. Laying of foundation stone for Bayreuth opera house.

1873 Publication of first *Untimely Meditation* (on David Strauss).

1874 Publication of second and third *Untimely Meditations* (*On the Use and Disadvantage of History* and *Schopenhauer as Educator*).

1875 Meets musician Heinrich Köselitz (Peter Gast).

1876 Publication of fourth *Untimely Meditation* (on Wagner). Attends first Bayreuth Festival. Signs of estrangement from

Wagner culminating in their final meeting in October. Beginning of friendship with psychologist Paul Rée. As a result of illness, granted convalescent leave from university.

1878 Publication of *Human All Too Human*, Part I. End of friendship with Wagners.

1879 Retires from teaching on grounds of ill health, receives sick pension for next six years.

1880 Publication of *The Wanderer and his Shadow*, *Human All Too Human*, Part II. First stay in Venice. First winter in Genoa.

1881 Publication of *Daybreak*. First summer in Sils-Maria. First hears Bizet's *Carmen* in Genoa.

1882 Publication of *The Gay Science*. Meets Lou Andreas Salomé, proposes marriage via Paul Rée and is refused.

1883 Publication of *Thus Spake Zarathustra*, Parts I and II. Death of Wagner.

1884 Publication of *Thus Spake Zarathustra*, Part III.

1885 Private printing of *Thus Spake Zarathustra*, Part IV. Estrangement from sister Elisabeth who marries anti-Semite and colonizing activist Bernhard Förster.

1886 Publication of *Beyond Good and Evil*. Second editions (with new prefaces) of *The Birth of Tragedy* and *Human, All Too Human*.

1887 Publication of *On the Genealogy of Morals*. Second editions (with new prefaces) of *Daybreak, The Gay Science, Thus Spake Zarathustra*, Parts I–III.

1888 First stay in Turin. Georg Brandes lectures on Nietzsche at the University of Copenhagen. Publication of *The Wagner Case*. Completion of *Dionysus Dithyrambs, The Antichrist, Ecce Homo, Nietzsche contra Wagner*. Begins to write a series of increasingly disturbing letters to friends and public figures. Inauguration of the Försters' Nueva Germania colony in Paraguay.

1889 Publication of *Twilight of the Idols*. Mental breakdown in Turin. Overbeck brings Nietzsche back from Italy. Stay in psychiatric clinic at University of Jena. Death of Bernhard Förster in Paraguay.

1890 Nietzsche discharged into mother's care in Naumberg.

1891 Publication of the *Dionysus Dithyrambs*. Elisabeth publishes Bernhard Förster's *Colony of New Germany in Paraguay*.

1894 Publication of *The Antichrist*. Elisabeth founds the Nietzsche Archive in Naumberg (transferring it to Weimar two years later).

1895 Publication of *Nietzsche contra Wagner*. Elisabeth publishes *The Life of Friedrich Nietzsche*, Volume I.

1897 On the death of their mother, Elisabeth moves Nietzsche to Weimar, where he lives until his death. Elisabeth publishes *The Life of Friedrich Nietzsche*, Volume II, Part I.

1900 Death of Friedrich Nietzsche on 25 August.

1901 Publication of *The Will to Power*, fragments from posthumous papers selected by Elisabeth and Peter Gast.

1904 Elisabeth publishes *The Life of Friedrich Nietzsche*, Volume II, Part II.

1906 Second expanded edition of *The Will to Power*.

1908 Publication of *Ecce Homo*.

1912 Elisabeth publishes *The Young Nietzsche*.

1914 Elisabeth publishes *The Lonely Nietzsche*.

1933 Hitler visits Nietzsche Archive at Elisabeth's invitation, is presented with Nietzsche's walking stick and an anti-Semitic tract by Bernhard Förster.

1935 Death of Elisabeth Nietzsche.

1967 Publication of first full chronological edition (Colli–Montinari) of Nietzsche's works.

ON THE GENEALOGY OF MORALS

A Polemic

PREFACE

1

We remain unknown to ourselves,* we seekers after knowledge, even to ourselves: and with good reason. We have never sought after ourselves*—so how should we one day find ourselves? It has rightly been said that: 'Where your treasure is, there will your heart be also';* *our* treasure is to be found in the beehives of knowledge. As spiritual bees from birth, this is our eternal destination, our hearts are set on one thing only—'bringing something home'. Whatever else life has to offer, so-called 'experiences'—who among us is serious enough for them? Or has enough time for them? In such matters, we were, I fear, never properly 'abreast of things': our heart is just not in it—nor, if it comes to it, are our ears! Imagine someone who, when woken suddenly from divine distraction and self-absorption by the twelve loud strokes of the noon bell, asks himself: 'What time is it?' In much the same way, we rub our ears *after the fact* and ask in complete surprise and embarrassment: '*What* was that we just experienced?', or even 'Who *are* we really?' Then we count back over in retrospect, as I said, every one of the twelve trembling strokes of our experience, our life, our *being*—and alas! lose our count in the process... And so we necessarily remain a mystery to ourselves, we fail to understand ourselves, we are *bound* to mistake ourselves. Our eternal sentence reads: 'Everyone is furthest from himself'*—of ourselves, we have no knowledge...

2

—My thoughts on the *origin* of our moral prejudices—for such is the subject of this polemic—found their first, spare, provisional expression in the collection of aphorisms entitled *Human, All Too Human: A Book for Free Spirits*. I began writing that book in Sorrento, during a winter which allowed me to make a halt, as a walker makes a halt, and to survey the distant and dangerous expanse through which my mind had been making its way up until then. This was in the winter of 1876–7; the thoughts themselves are older. For the most part, I take up the same thoughts in these present essays—let us hope that they have thrived since then, that they have matured, grown brighter, stronger, more complete! But *that* I still hold to these ideas today, and that they themselves have since become increasingly inseparable, indeed have even grown into one another and become intertwined—all this strengthens my happy assurance that, far from emerging as isolated, random, or sporadic phenomena, these ideas grew from a common root, from a *fundamental will* of knowledge, a will which issued its imperatives from the depths, speaking in increasingly definite terms and demanding increasingly definite answers. For nothing else befits a philosopher. We have no right to any *isolated* act whatsoever: to make isolated errors and to discover isolated truths are equally forbidden us. Rather, our thoughts, our values, our yeses and noes and ifs and whethers grow out of us with the same necessity with which a tree bears its fruits—all related and connected to one another and evidence of a *single* will, a *single* health, a *single* earth, a *single* sun.—And as to whether these fruits of ours are to *your* taste?—But what is that to the trees! What is that to *us*, the philosophers!...

3

I harbour a particular reservation which I am reluctant to confess—for it concerns *morality*, everything which has up to now been celebrated as morality—a reservation which emerged so unsolicited, so early and inexorably, so in contradiction with my environment, age, models, and origins, that I might almost be entitled to call it my 'A priori'.* As to the nature of this reservation—I found that my curiosity and suspicion were soon drawn up short at the question of the real *origin* of our notions of good and evil. In fact, as a 13-year-old boy I was already preoccupied with the problem of the origin of evil. At an age when one has 'half children's games and half God at heart',* I devoted my first literary piece of child's play, my first exercise in philosophical writing to this subject—and as for my 'solution' to the problem at that time, I gave God the honour, as is fitting, and made him the father of *evil*. Was *this* the very thing which my 'A priori' required of me? That new immoral, or at least amoral, 'A priori' and the alas! so anti-Kantian, so enigmatic 'categorical imperative'* which spoke through it and to which I have since been increasingly attentive and more than just attentive?... Fortunately, I have since learnt to separate theology from morality and ceased looking for the origin of evil *behind* the world. Some schooling in history and philology, together with an innate sense of discrimination with respect to questions of psychology, quickly transformed my problem into another one: under what conditions did man invent the value-judgements good and evil? *And what value do they themselves possess?* Have they helped or hindered the progress of mankind? Are they a sign of indigence, of impoverishment, of the degeneration of life? Or do they rather reveal the plenitude, the strength, the will of life, its courage, confidence, and future?—To these questions, I found several audacious answers. I distinguished between periods, peoples, degrees of rank among individuals, I narrowed down my problem. Out of the answers grew new questions, investigations, hypotheses, probabilities: until finally I had a land of my own, a soil of my own, a completely unknown, burgeoning, flourishing world, like a secret garden, whose existence no one had been allowed to suspect... Oh how *fortunate* we are, we seekers after knowledge, provided only that we do not break our silence prematurely!...

4

The first impetus to give expression to some of my hypotheses on the origin of morality came from a neat and tidy little book, clever even to the point of precociousness. There for the first time I clearly encountered an inverted and perverted kind of genealogical hypothesis, the genuinely *English* kind, and found myself drawn to it—as opposites attract one another. The title of this little book was *The Origin of Moral Sensations*; its author Dr Paul Rée;* the year of its appearance 1877. It is possible that I have never read anything which I have rejected so thoroughly, proposition by proposition, conclusion by conclusion, as this book: but without the least ill humour and impatience. In the aforementioned work on which I was engaged at that time, I referred, both appropriately and inappropriately, to the propositions of this book, not in order to refute them—what interest have I in refutations!—but rather, as befits a positive spirit, in order to replace an improbability with something more probable, and occasionally even to replace one error with another. At that time, as I said, I first brought to light those hypotheses on the genealogy of morals to which these present essays are devoted. I did so clumsily, as I would be the first to admit to myself, in a manner still constrained, still without my own particular language for these particular things and with much backsliding and hesitation. In specific terms, compare what I say in *Human, All Too Human*, §45 on the dual prehistory of good and evil (that is, in the noble and servile spheres); likewise, in §136 on the value of ascetic morality; likewise, in §§96 and 99 and in *Mixed Opinions and Sayings*, §89 on the 'morality of custom', that much older and more original kind of morality which lies worlds apart from the altruistic method of evaluation (in which Dr Rée, like all English genealogists of morals, sees the moral method of evaluation *as such*); likewise §92, *The Wanderer*, §26, and *Daybreak*, §112 on the origin of justice as a compromise between those who are approximately equal in power (equality as the condition of all contracts, and consequently of all law)—; likewise, *The Wanderer*, §§22 and 33 on the origin of punishment, for which the aim of deterrence is neither essential nor original (as Dr Rée thinks—it is rather only introduced later, under specific conditions, and always as something incidental, something supplementary).

5

At that particular moment, my real concern was with something much more important than my own or anyone else's hypotheses about the origin of morality (or, to be more precise: the latter interest was completely subordinate to a single goal, to which it is merely one among many means). For me, what was at stake was the *value* of morality—and on that question I had no choice but to engage almost single-handedly with my great teacher Schopenhauer.* That book of mine, its passion and its secret refutation, was addressed to him, as to a contemporary (—for that book too was a 'polemic'). At issue was the value of the 'unegoistic', the instincts of compassion, self-abnegation, self-sacrifice, those very instincts which Schopenhauer had for so long made golden, godly, and transcendent, until finally they became for him 'values in themselves', on the basis of which he *said no* to life and also to himself. But it was against *these* very instincts that an increasingly fundamental suspicion, a scepticism which dug ever deeper, spoke out within me! It was here that I saw the *great* danger for mankind, its most sublime temptation and seduction—leading in what direction? towards nothingness?—It was here that I saw the beginning of the end, the stagnation, the tired nostalgia, the will turning *against* life, the melancholy and tender signs of the approach of the last illness. I regarded the inexorable progress of the morality of compassion, which afflicted even the philosophers with its illness, as the most sinister* symptom of the sinister development of our European culture, as its detour leading in what direction? Towards a new Buddhism?* towards a European Buddhism? towards—*nihilism*?...* For the modern predilection for compassion, its overestimation in philosophy, is a recent development: the very *worthlessness* of compassion was formerly a point of agreement among philosophers. To mention only Plato, Spinoza, La Rochefoucauld, and Kant,* four minds as different from one another as possible, but united in one respect: in their contempt for compassion.—

6

This problem of the *value* of compassion and of the morality of compassion (—I am an opponent of the shameful modern weakening of sensibility—) seems at first merely an isolated issue, a free-standing question-mark. But whoever pauses here, whoever *learns* to ask questions here, will undergo the same experience as I—that of a huge new prospect opening up, a vertiginous possibility, as every kind of mistrust, suspicion, and fear leaps forward, and the belief in morality, all morality, falters. Finally, a new demand finds expression. Let us articulate this *new demand*: we stand in need of a *critique* of moral values, *the value of these values itself should first of all be called into question*. This requires a knowledge of the conditions and circumstances of their growth, development, and displacement (morality as consequence, symptom, mask, Tartufferie,* illness, misunderstanding: but also morality as cause, cure, stimulant, inhibition, poison); knowledge the like of which has never before existed nor even been desired. The *value* of these 'values' was accepted as given, as fact, as beyond all question. Previously, no one had expressed even the remotest doubt or shown the slightest hesitation in assuming the 'good man' to be of greater worth than the 'evil man', of greater worth in the sense of his usefulness in promoting the progress of human *existence* (including the future of man). What? And if the opposite were the case? What? What if there existed a symptom of regression in the 'good man', likewise a danger, a temptation, a poison, a narcotic, by means of which the present were living *at the expense of the future*? Perhaps more comfortably and less dangerously, but also in less grand style, in a humbler manner?... So that none other than morality itself would be the culprit, if the *highest power and splendour* of the human type, in itself a possibility, were never to be reached? So that morality would constitute the danger of dangers?...

7

Suffice it to say that, since this prospect opened up before me, I myself had reason to look around for learned, daring, and hardworking colleagues (I continue to do so). What is involved is a journey across the wide expanse of morality, so distant and so inaccessible—morality which has actually existed, which has actually been lived—a journey with nothing but new questions and with fresh eyes, as it were: does this not amount practically to *discovering* this expanse of territory for the first time?... If in the process the aforementioned Dr Rée came to mind, among others, this was because I had no doubt that he would be bound by the very nature of his questions to develop a more correct method of arriving at the answers. Have I been mistaken? I wished in any case to point such a sharp and impartial eye in a better direction, the direction of the real *history of morality*, and to warn him off in good time from such English hypothesizing *into the blue*. For there is clearly another colour which ought to be a hundred times more important to a genealogist of morals: that is, *grey*—by that I mean what has been documented, what is really ascertainable, what has really existed, in short, the whole long hieroglyphic text, so difficult to decipher, of humanity's moral past!—*This* remained unknown to Dr Rée; but he *had* read Darwin*—and so in his hypotheses, and in a way which is entertaining at least, the Darwinian beast civilly extends a hand to the morally meek and mild, the ultra-modern soul who has learnt 'not to bite'. In the latter's expression a certain good-humoured and refined indolence is joined by a grain of pessimism and fatigue: as if all these things—the problems of morality—were really not worth taking so seriously. On the contrary, it seems to me now that there is nothing which better *repays* serious consideration: to such rewards belong for example the possibility of one day being entitled to approach the problems of morality *in high spirits*. For high spirits, or, to put it in my own words, *gay science**—is a reward: a reward for a long, bold, hard-working, and subterranean seriousness, which is not to everyone's taste, admittedly. But on the day when we say with full hearts: 'Onwards! our old morality is part of the *comedy* too!', on that day we will have discovered a new plot and potential for the Dionysian drama* of the *'Fate of the Soul'*—: and one which that grand old eternal comic poet of our existence will exploit, on that you may depend!...

8

—If this text strikes anyone as unintelligible and far from easy listening, the blame, as I see it, does not necessarily rest with me. The text is clear enough, assuming in the first place, as I do, that one has put some effort into reading my earlier writings: for these do, in fact, present difficulties. To take my '*Zarathustra*',* for instance, only someone whom its every word had at some time deeply wounded and on another occasion just as deeply delighted might in my view claim a real knowledge of it: for only then he might enjoy the privilege of sharing reverently in the halcyonic element out of which that work was born, in its solar brightness, distance, breadth, and certainty. In other cases, the aphoristic form presents problems: this stems from the fact that nowadays this form is not taken *seriously enough*. An aphorism, honestly cast and stamped, is still some way from being 'deciphered' once it has been read; rather, it is only then that its *interpretation* can begin, and for this an art of interpretation is required. In the third essay of this book I have offered a model for what I mean by 'interpretation' in such a case—the essay opens with an aphorism and is itself a commentary upon it. Admittedly, to practise reading as an *art* in this way requires one thing above all, and it is something which today more than ever has been thoroughly unlearnt—a fact which explains why it will be some time before my writings are 'readable'—it is something for which one must be practically bovine and certainly *not* a 'modern man': that is to say, *rumination*...*

Sils-Maria, Upper Engadine, July 1887

FIRST ESSAY

'Good and Evil', 'Good and Bad'

1

—These English psychologists,* to whom we owe the only attempts so far to develop a history of the genesis of morality, themselves present us with an enigma. As living and breathing enigmas, this gives them, I confess, an essential advantage over their books—*they themselves are interesting*! These English psychologists—what are they really after? Whether by accident or design, they are always to be found at the same task—pushing to the forefront the *partie honteuse** of our inner world, seeking the real directing force of human development, the real decisive influence upon it, in the very place where the intellectual pride of man would least *wish* to find it (for example, in the *vis inertiae** of habit or in forgetfulness or in the blind arbitrariness of a mechanistic chain of ideas, or in something purely passive, automatic, reflex-like, molecular, and fundamentally stupid). What drives these psychologists always in *this* particular direction? Is it a secret, spiteful, vulgar, and perhaps unacknowledged instinct to belittle man? Or perhaps a pessimistic suspicion, the mistrust of disappointed, gloomy idealists who have turned green and poisonous? Or a petty, subterranean, rancorous hostility towards Christianity (and Plato),* which may not even have crossed the threshold of consciousness? Or even a lascivious taste for an irritant, the painful paradox, for the questionable and absurd aspects of life? Or finally, a little of all these: a little vulgarity, a little gloom, a little anti-Christianity, a little itch and need for spice?... But I am told that they are simply cold, boring old frogs who crawl around and hop into people, as though they were completely in their element, that is, in a *quagmire*. I hear this with reluctance—indeed, I do not believe it, and if one may wish where one cannot know, then I wish heartily that the opposite were the case—that these microscopic researchers of the soul were basically brave, generous, and proud animals, who know how to restrain their emotions as well as their pain, and have taught themselves to sacrifice all wishfulness to truth, to *every* truth, even the simple, bitter, ugly, repulsive, unChristian, immoral truth... For such truths do exist.—

2

So the greatest respect to the good spirits who preside over these historians of morality! Unfortunately, there is no doubt that they lack the *historical spirit*, that they have been abandoned by all the good spirits of history! As is the wont of philosophers, they all think in an *essentially* unhistorical manner; there is no doubt about that. The amateurishness of their genealogy of morals comes to light as soon as they have to account for the origin of 'good' as concept and judgement. 'Originally'—so they decree—'unegoistic actions were acclaimed and described as good by those towards whom they were directed, thus those to whom they were *useful*. The origin of this acclaim was later forgotten and unegoistic actions were simply felt to be good, because they were *habitually* always praised as such—as if they were in themselves something good.' It is clear from the outset that all the typical characteristics of the English psychologists' prejudice are already present in this first deduction—here we have 'utility', 'forgetting', 'habit', and finally 'error', all as the basis of a value-judgement which has up to now been the pride of civilized man and been accepted as a kind of essential human prerogative. The *goal* here is to humble this pride, devalue this value-judgement: is this goal attained?... It seems clear to me that this theory looks in the wrong place for the real origin of the concept 'good'. The judgement 'good' does *not* derive from those to whom 'goodness' is shown! Rather, the 'good' themselves—that is, the noble, the powerful, the superior, and the high-minded—were the ones who felt themselves and their actions to be good—that is, as of the first rank—and posited them as such, in contrast to everything low, low-minded, common, and plebeian. On the basis of this *pathos of distance*,* they first arrogated the right to create values, to coin the names of values.

What did utility matter to them? The point of view of utility could not be more alien and inappropriate to such a high-temperature outpouring of the highest value-judgements when engaged in the making and breaking of hierarchies: for here feeling is at the opposite end of the scale from the low temperature presupposed by every prudent calculation and utilitarian estimation—and not only on one occasion, not for an exceptional hour, but over the long term. As I said, the pathos of nobility and distance, the enduring, dominating, and fundamental overall feeling of a higher ruling kind in relation to a lower kind, to a 'below'—*that* is the origin of the opposition between 'good' and 'bad'. (The right of the masters to confer names extends so far that one should allow oneself to grasp the origin of language itself as the expression of the power of the rulers: they say 'this *is* such and such', they put their seal on each thing and event with a sound and in the process take possession of it.) It follows from this origin that there is from the outset absolutely *no* necessary connection between the word 'good' and 'unegoistic' actions, as the superstition of the genealogists of morals would have it. Rather, it is only with the decline of aristocratic value-judgements that this whole opposition between 'egoistic' and 'unegoistic' comes to impose itself increasingly on the human conscience. To adopt my own terminology, it is the *herd-instinct*, which here finally has its chance to put in a word (and to put itself into *words*). Even then, it is a long time before this instinct dominates to such an extent that the moral value-judgement catches and sticks fast on this opposition (as is, for example, the case in contemporary Europe: today the prejudice which takes 'moral', 'unegoistic', '*désintéressé*'* as synonyms already rules with the power of an '*idée fixe*' and mental illness.)

3

As a second point, however: quite apart from its untenability in historical terms, this hypothesis on the origin of the value-judgement 'good' suffers from an inherent psychological contradiction. The acclaim which the unegoistic action receives is supposedly derived from its utility, and this origin has supposedly been *forgotten*—but how is such forgetting even *possible*? Have such actions at some point perhaps ceased to be useful? The opposite is the case: their utility has become rather the daily experience for all time, something which has been continually underlined anew, and, consequently, instead of disappearing from consciousness, instead of becoming forgettable, must have impressed itself on consciousness with ever-greater clarity. How much more reasonable is the opposing theory (which is no more true for all that—), represented by Herbert Spencer,* for example. Spencer postulates that the concept 'good' is essentially the same as the concept 'useful' or 'expedient', so that humanity has summed up and sanctioned precisely its *unforgotten* and *unforgettable* experiences of what is useful and expedient on the one hand and what is harmful and inexpedient on the other in the judgements 'good' and 'bad'. According to this theory, whatever has proven itself useful from time immemorial is good: as a result, it may assert its validity as 'of the highest value', as 'valuable in itself'. This mode of explanation is, as I said, also incorrect, but at least the explanation itself is internally consistent and tenable in terms of its psychology.

4

—What pointed me in the *right* direction was actually the question of what the designations of 'good' coined in various languages meant from an etymological perspective.* I found that they all led back to the *same transformation of concepts*—that 'refined' or 'noble' in the sense of social standing is everywhere the fundamental concept, from which 'good' in the sense of 'having a refined soul', 'noble' in the sense of 'superior in soul', 'privileged in soul' necessarily developed. This development always ran parallel with that other one by means of which 'common' or 'plebeian' or 'low' ultimately slide over into the concept 'bad'. The most eloquent example of this latter process is the German word *schlecht* [bad] itself—it is identical with *schlicht* [simple] (compare *schlechtweg*, *schlechterdings* [simply]),* and originally designated the simple common man in straightforward contrast to the noble man, without at that time implying a suspicious sideward glance on the part of the speaker. Roughly around the time of the Thirty Years War*—late enough, then—this sense was displaced to produce the one which is usual now.—This seems to me to be a *fundamental* insight with respect to the genealogy of morals. The reason for its coming to light so late is the inhibiting influence exerted in the modern world by the democratic prejudice against all questions of origin. And this prejudice encroaches even on what are apparently the most objective areas of natural science and physiology, which I shall only allude to here. But the degree of mischief which this prejudice can cause, particularly in matters of ethics and history, once it has been unleashed and allowed to develop into hatred, is shown by the notorious case of Buckle.* There once again the *plebeian nature* of the modern mind, which is of English origin, broke out on its native soil, with the intensity of a muddy volcano and with the same over-salted, over-loud, common garrulousness with which all volcanoes have previously held forth.

5

With respect to *our* problem—which might with good reason be described as a *reticent* problem, one which addresses itself with discrimination to a few ears only—it is of no small interest to note that, in those words and roots which designate 'good', the main nuance, according to which the noble felt themselves to be men of higher rank, often still shows through. Admittedly, the most frequent practice is perhaps for those of higher rank to name themselves according to their superiority in matters of power (as 'the powerful', 'the masters', 'those who command'), or according to the most visible sign of this superiority, as, for example, 'the wealthy', 'the owners' (that is the meaning of *arya*;* and similar formulations can be found in Persian and Slavic). But they also do so according to a *typical character trait*: and this is the case which concerns us here. The noble might refer to themselves, for example, as 'the truthful': the prime example is the Greek nobility, whose spokesman is the Megarian poet Theognis.* The word coined for this purpose—*esthlos**—means according to its root someone who *is*, who has reality, who is real, who is true. Then, with a subjective turn, the true becomes the truthful: in this phase of concept-transformation the word becomes the slogan and motto of the nobility and slides completely over into the meaning 'noble', marking it off from the *deceitful* common man, as Theognis takes and represents him—until finally, after the decline of the nobility, the word survives to designate nobility of soul and becomes at the same time ripe and sweet. In the word *kakos*,* as in *deilos** (the plebeian in contrast to *agathos**), cowardliness is emphasized: perhaps this gives an indication of the direction in which the etymological origin of *agathos*, with its multiple meanings, is to be sought. In the Latin *malus** (to which I juxtapose *melas**), the common man may be designated as having dark skin, above all, dark hair ('*hic niger est*'*), as the pre-Aryan inhabitant of Italian soil, who was through colour most clearly distinguished from the blond, that is, Aryan, race of conquerors who had come to power. At least, Gaelic offered me an exactly corresponding case—*fin* (for example, in the name *Fin-Gal**), the word characterizing the nobility, which ultimately meant the good, the noble, the pure, but originally the blond-headed, in contrast to the swarthy, dark-haired original inhabitants. The Celts, incidentally, were a thoroughly blond race: it is a mistake to relate those areas of essentially dark-haired population, which are to be seen on the more carefully researched ethnographic maps of Germany, to any sort of Celtic origin and miscegenation, as Virchow* still does. Rather, it is the *pre-Aryan* population of Germany which shows through in these places. (The same is true for almost the whole of Europe: essentially, the subjugated race has ultimately regained the upper hand, in colour, size of skull, perhaps even in the intellectual and social instincts. Who can say whether modern democracy, the even more recent phenomenon of anarchism, and particularly that tendency, now common to all European socialists, towards the '*commune*',* the most primitive form of society, does not for the most part represent a huge *atavistic throwback*—and that the race of conquerors and *masters*, the Aryan race, now finds itself physiologically in an inferior position?...) I believe that I am entitled to interpret the

Latin *bonus** as 'warrior': provided that I correctly derive *bonus* from the older *duonus* (compare *bellum** = *duellum* = *duenlum*, in which *duonus* seems to me to be included). So *bonus* as a man of conflict, of division (*duo*), as warrior: from this it is clear in what a man's 'goodness' consisted in ancient Rome. Our German *gut* [good] itself: should it not mean 'the godly' [*den Göttlichen*], the man 'of godly race' [*göttlichen Geschlechts*]? And should it not be identical with the Goths [*Goten*],* the name of the people (and originally of the nobility)? The grounds for this hypothesis would be out of place here.—

6

To the rule that the political concept of rank always transforms itself into a spiritual concept of rank, it at first constitutes no exception (although it may in turn occasion such exceptions) if the highest caste is at the same time the *priestly* caste, and consequently prefers to designate itself collectively through a predicate which reminds one of its priestly function. It is here, for example, that 'pure' and 'impure' are first opposed as marks of social station; and here also that a 'good' and a 'bad' are later developed in a sense which is no longer one of social station. By the way, one should be warned against taking these concepts of 'pure' and 'impure' too seriously, too broadly, or even symbolically from the outset: rather, all human concepts from earlier times were, to an extent which we can scarcely conceive, initially understood in a crude, clumsy, external, narrow, and frankly, particularly *unsymbolic* way. The 'pure' man is from the outset merely a man who washes, who denies himself certain types of food which cause skin complaints, who refrains from sleeping with the unclean women of the lower classes, who abhors blood—and no more, not a great deal more than that! On the other hand, admittedly, the whole constitution of an essentially priestly aristocracy illuminates why it should be here rather than anywhere else that the dangerous internalization and intensification of the value-oppositions could take place at an early stage. In fact, these oppositions have finally torn open chasms between man and man, chasms which would make even an Achilles of spiritual freedom shudder before he leapt. There is from the outset something *unhealthy* in such priestly aristocracies and in the customs which prevail among them, customs which are turned away from action and combine brooding with emotional volatility. The consequence of these customs is the almost unavoidable intestinal sickness and neurasthenia which afflicts priests of all times. But as for what they themselves invented as a cure for their sickliness—are we not bound to say that its after-effects have ultimately proven to be a hundred times more dangerous than the illness which it was intended to relieve? Mankind itself continues to suffer from the after-effects of these naïve priestly cures! Let us think, for example, of certain forms of diet (avoidance of meat), of fasting, of sexual abstinence, of flight 'into the desert' (Weir Mitchell's isolation therapy,* admittedly without the accompanying fattening diet and over-eating, which constitutes the most effective remedy to all the hysteria* of the ascetic ideal). And added to that, the whole anti-sensual and enervating metaphysics of the priests, their self-hypnosis in the manner of fakirs and Brahmins—Brahma* used as a crystal ball and *idée fixe*—and the ultimate, only too understandable general satiety with its radical cure, with *nothingness* (or God—the desire for a *unio mystica** with God is the Buddhist's desire for nothingness, nirvana*—and nothing more!). With the priests, *everything* becomes more dangerous, not only cures and therapies, but also arrogance, revenge, perspicacity, extravagance, love, the desire to dominate, virtue, illness. With some fairness, admittedly, it might also be added that it is only on the basis of this *essentially dangerous* form of human existence, the priestly form, that man has at all developed into an *interesting animal*, that it is only here that the human soul has in a higher sense taken on *depth* and become *evil*—and these have certainly been the two fundamental forms of man's superiority over other animals up to now!...

7

—By now it will be clear how easily the priestly mode of evaluation may diverge from the knightly-aristocratic mode and then develop into its opposite. This process receives a particular impetus each time the priest and warrior castes jealously confront each other and are unwilling to strike a compromise. The knightly-aristocratic value-judgements presuppose a powerful physicality, a rich, burgeoning, even overflowing health, as well as all those things which help to preserve it—war, adventure, hunting, dancing, competitive games, and everything which involves strong, free, high-spirited activity. As we have seen, the noble priestly mode of evaluation has different conditions: so much the worse for the priests when it comes to war! Priests are, as is well-known, the *most evil enemies*—but why? Because they are the most powerless. From powerlessness their hatred grows to take on a monstrous and sinister shape, the most cerebral and most poisonous form. The very greatest haters of world-history have always been priests, as have the most ingenious. In comparison with the ingenuity of priestly revenge, all other intelligence scarcely merits consideration. Human history would be a much too stupid affair were it not for the intelligence introduced by the powerless. Let us immediately consider the most important example. Nothing which anyone else has perpetrated against the 'noble', the 'powerful', the 'masters', the 'rulers' merits discussion in comparison with the deeds of the *Jews*—the Jews, that priestly people who ultimately knew no other way of exacting satisfaction from its enemies and conquerors than through a radical transvaluation of their values, through an art of *the most intelligent revenge*. This was only as befitted a priestly people, the people of the most downtrodden priestly vindictiveness. It has been the Jews who have, with terrifying consistency, dared to undertake the reversal of the aristocratic value equation (good = noble = powerful = beautiful = happy = blessed) and have held on to it tenaciously by the teeth of the most unfathomable hatred (the hatred of the powerless). It is they who have declared: 'The miserable alone are the good; the poor, the powerless, the low alone are the good. The suffering, the deprived, the sick, the ugly are the only pious ones, the only blessed, for them alone is there salvation. You, on the other hand, the noble and the powerful, you are for all eternity the evil, the cruel, the lascivious, the insatiable, the godless ones. You will be without salvation, accursed and damned to all eternity!' There is no doubt as to *who* inherited this Jewish transvaluation...* In relation to the monstrous initiative, disastrous beyond all bounds, which the Jews have taken with this most fundamental of all declarations of war, I remind the reader of the phrase which I arrived at in another context (*Beyond Good and Evil*, §195): that with the Jews *the slave revolt in morals** begins: that revolt which has a two-thousand-year history behind it and which has today dropped out of sight only because it—has succeeded...

8

—But you are finding this hard to follow? You have no eyes for something which took two thousand years to triumph?... That comes as no surprise: all things whose *history stretches out far behind them* are difficult to see, to see in their entirety. But *this* is indeed what happened: from the trunk of that tree of revenge and hatred, Jewish hatred—the deepest and most sublime hatred, that is, the kind of hatred which creates ideals and changes the meaning of values, a hatred the like of which has never been on earth—from this tree grew forth something equally incomparable, a *new love*, the deepest and most sublime of all the kinds of love—and from what other trunk could it have grown?... But let no one think that it somehow grew up as the genuine negation of that thirst for revenge, as the antithesis of Jewish hatred! No, the opposite is the case! Love grew forth from this hatred, as its crown, as its triumphant crown, spreading itself ever wider in the purest brightness and fullness of the sun, as a crown which pursued in the lofty realm of light the goals of hatred—victory, spoils, seduction—driven there by the same impulse with which the roots of that hatred sank down ever further and more lasciviously into everything deep and evil. This Jesus of Nazareth, as the gospel of love incarnate, this 'redeemer' bringing victory and salvation to the poor, the sick, the sinners—did he not represent the most sinister and irresistible form of the very same temptation, the indirect temptation to accept those self-same *Jewish* values and new versions of the ideal? Has Israel not reached the ultimate goal of its sublime vindictiveness through the detour of this very 'redeemer' who appeared to oppose and announce the dissolution of Israel? Is it not characteristic of the secret black art of a truly *great* policy of revenge, of a far-sighted, subterranean revenge which unfolds itself slowly and thinks ahead, that Israel itself was obliged to deny the very instrument of this revenge as a mortal enemy and crucify him before the whole world, so that the 'whole world', all the opponents of Israel, might unthinkingly bite on just this very bait? And on the other hand, would it be possible, with the most refined ingenuity, to devise a *more dangerous* bait? To devise something which could even approach the seductive, intoxicating, anaesthetizing, and corrupting power of that symbol of the 'holy cross', that horrific paradox of the 'crucified God', that mystery of an inconceivably ultimate, most extreme cruelty and self-crucifixion undertaken *for the salvation of mankind*?... It is certain at least that *sub hoc signo** Israel's revenge and transvaluation of all values has so far continued to triumph over all other ideals, over all *nobler* ideals.— —

9

—'But why do you persist in talking about *nobler* ideals? Let us stick to the facts: the people have won—or the "slaves" or the "plebeians" or the "herd" or whatever you want to call them—and if the Jews brought this about, then so much the better! Never in world history did a people have a more important mission. The "masters" are done away with; the morality of the common man has won. This victory might also be seen as a form of blood-poisoning (it has mixed the races together)—I shall not contradict that; but there is no doubt that the toxin has *succeeded*. The "redemption" of humanity (from the "masters", that is) is proceeding apace; everything is visibly becoming more Jewish or Christian or plebeian (what does the terminology matter!). The progress of this poison through the entire body of mankind seems inexorable. From now on, its pace may even be slower, finer, less audible, more considered—there is no hurry, after all... Does the Church still have a *necessary* role to play in this respect, does it still have a right to existence at all? Or could it be dispensed with? *Quaeritur*.*

Does it seem to hinder rather than help the advance of this poison? Now this is exactly where its potential usefulness lies... Certainly, the Church remains something crude and uncouth, repulsive to a more delicate intellect, to a really modern taste. Ought it not at least to refine itself a little?... The Church today is more likely to alienate than to seduce... Who among us would be a free spirit if it were not for the existence of the Church? It is the Church which we find repellent, *not* its poison... The Church aside, we too love its poison...'—Such is the epilogue to my speech provided by a 'free spirit', an honest animal, as he has amply demonstrated, and a democrat, moreover; he had been listening to me until now and could not bear to hear me keep silent. For on this matter, there is much to keep silent about.—

10

—The slave revolt in morals begins when *ressentiment** itself becomes creative and ordains values: the *ressentiment* of creatures to whom the real reaction, that of the deed, is denied and who find compensation in an imaginary revenge. While all noble morality grows from a triumphant affirmation of itself, slave morality from the outset says no to an 'outside', to an 'other', to a 'non-self': and *this* no is its creative act. The reversal of the evaluating gaze—this *necessary* orientation outwards rather than inwards to the self—belongs characteristically to *ressentiment*. In order to exist at all, slave morality from the outset always needs an opposing, outer world; in physiological terms, it needs external stimuli in order to act—its action is fundamentally reaction. The opposite is the case with the aristocratic mode of evaluation: this acts and grows spontaneously, it only seeks out its antithesis in order to affirm itself more thankfully and more joyfully. Its negative concept, 'low', 'common', 'bad', is only a derived, pale contrast to its positive basic concept which is thoroughly steeped in life and passion—'we the noble, we the good, we the beautiful, we the happy ones!' If the aristocratic mode of evaluation errs and sins against reality, this happens in relation to the sphere with which it is *not* sufficiently familiar, and against real knowledge of which it stubbornly defends itself: it misjudges on occasion the sphere it despises—that of the common man, of the lower people. On the other hand, one may consider that this feeling of contempt, condescension, and superiority, granted that it *falsifies* the image of those despised, will trail far behind the falsification by means of which the downtrodden hatred, the revenge of the powerless will attack its opponent—*in effigie*,* of course. There is, in fact, too much nonchalance, too much levity, too much distraction and impatience, even too much good temper mixed up with this aristocratic contempt for it to be capable of transforming its object into a real caricature and monster. One should not fail to notice the almost benevolent *nuances* present in all the words with which the Greek nobility distinguishes the lower people from itself; how a kind of pity, consideration, and forbearance continually intervenes and sweetens, until ultimately almost all the words applied to the common man survive as expressions meaning 'unhappy', 'pitiable' (compare *deilos*, *delaios*, *poneros*, *mochtheros*,* the last two designating the common man as working slave and beast of burden)—and how, too, 'bad', 'low', 'unhappy' have never since ceased to ring in a *single* note to the Greek ear, with a tonality in which 'unhappy' predominates. This is a legacy from the old, more noble, aristocratic mode of evaluation, which refuses to deny itself even in its contempt for others (—let me remind philologists in what sense *oizyros*, *anolbos*, *tlemon*, *dystychein*, *xymphora** were used). The 'well-bred' *felt* themselves to be 'the fortunate'; they did not have to construe their good fortune artificially through a glance at their enemies, to persuade themselves of it, to *convince themselves through lying* (as all men of *ressentiment* usually do). Likewise, as fully developed people overladen with strength, and consequently as *necessarily* active people, they knew better than to separate action from happiness—with them, activity is necessarily calculated into happiness (from where *eu prattein** takes its origin). All this is diametrically opposed to 'happiness' as understood on the level of the powerless, the oppressed, of those who suppurate with poisonous and hostile feelings, those for whom happiness appears essentially as narcotic, anaesthetic, calm, peace, 'sabbath', the expansion of feeling and the stretching of limbs, in a word, as *passivity*. While the noble man lives for himself in trust and openness (*gennaios** 'of noble birth' underlines the nuance of 'honest' and also 'naïve'), the man of *ressentiment* is neither upright nor naïve in his dealings with others, nor is he honest and open with himself. His soul *squints*; his mind loves bolt-holes, secret paths, back doors, he regards all hidden things as *his* world, *his* security, *his* refreshment; he has a perfect understanding of how to keep silent, how not to forget, how to wait, how to make himself provisionally small and submissive. A race of such men of *ressentiment* is bound in the end to become *cleverer* than any noble race, and it will respect cleverness to a completely different degree: that is, as a first condition of existence. In contrast, for aristocratic people cleverness easily acquires a delicate taste of luxury and refinement. They long considered cleverness less essential than the smooth functioning of their unconscious regulating instincts, than a certain recklessness, even. This latter took the form of a bold impetuosity, whether with respect to danger, the enemy, or the instantaneous outbursts of wrath, love, respect, gratitude, and revenge, by means of which noble souls have at all times recognized one another. For the *ressentiment* of the noble man himself, if it appears at all, completes and exhausts itself in an immediate reaction. For that reason, it does not *poison*. On the other hand, *ressentiment* simply fails to appear in countless cases where its emergence would be inevitable among the weak and the powerless. To be incapable of taking one's enemies, accidents, even one's *misdeeds* seriously for long—such is the sign of strong full natures, natures in possession of a surplus of the power to shape, form, and heal, of the power which also enables one to forget (a good example of this in the modern world is Mirabeau,* who had no memory for the insults and malicious behaviour directed against him and could not forgive simply because he could not—remember). Such a man with a *single* shrug shakes off much of that which worms and digs its way into others. Here alone is actual '*love* of one's enemy'* possible, assuming that such a thing is at all possible on earth. How much respect a noble man has already for his enemy!—and such respect is already a bridge to love... The noble man claims his enemy for himself, as a mark of distinction. He tolerates no other enemy than one in whom nothing is to be despised and a *great deal* is worthy of respect! In contrast, imagine the 'enemy' as conceived by the man of *ressentiment*. This is the very place where his deed, his creation is to be found—he has conceived the 'evil enemy', the '*evil man*'. Moreover, he has conceived him as a fundamental concept, from which he now derives another as an after-image and counterpart, the 'good man'—himself!...

11

This, then, is the very opposite of what the noble man does—for the latter conceives the fundamental concept 'good' spontaneously and in advance—that is, from his own point of view—and only then does he proceed to create for himself an idea of the 'bad'! This 'bad' of noble origin and that 'evil' which issues from the cauldron of insatiable hatred—the former being a retrospective creation, an incidental, a complementary colour, while the latter is the original, the beginning, the real *deed* in the conception of a slave morality—what a difference there is between these two words 'bad' and 'evil', in spite of the fact that they both appear to stand in opposition to one and the same concept of 'good'! But it is not the *same* concept of 'good' which is involved in each case: the question which should be asked is rather: *who* is actually 'evil' according to the morality of *ressentiment*? In all strictness, the answer is: *none other* than the 'good man' of the other morality, none other than the noble, powerful, dominating man, but only once he has been given a new colour, interpretation, and aspect by the poisonous eye of *ressentiment*. We would be the last to deny that anyone who met these 'good men' only as enemies would know them only as *evil enemies*, and that these same men, who are *inter pares** so strictly restrained by custom, respect, usage, gratitude, even more by circumspection and jealousy, and who in their relations with one another prove so inventive in matters of consideration, self-control, tenderness, fidelity, pride, and friendship—these same men behave towards the outside world—where the foreign, the *foreigners*, are to be found—in a manner not much better than predators on the rampage. There they enjoy freedom from all social constraint, in the wilderness they make up for the tension built up over a long period of confinement and enclosure within a peaceful community, they *regress* to the innocence of the predator's conscience, as rejoicing monsters, capable of high spirits as they walk away without qualms from a horrific succession of murder, arson, violence, and torture, as if it were nothing more than a student prank, something new for the poets to sing and celebrate for some time to come. There is no mistaking the predator beneath the surface of all these noble races, the magnificent *blond beast** roaming lecherously in search of booty and victory; the energy of this hidden core needs to be discharged from time to time, the animal must emerge again, must return to the wilderness—Roman, Arab, German, Japanese nobility, Homeric heroes, Scandinavian Vikings,—they all share this same need. The noble races are the ones who, wherever they have gone, have left the concept 'barbarian' in their wake; an awareness of this is betrayed even by their highest culture, which actually takes pride in it (for example, when Pericles* says to his Athenians in that famous funeral address, 'wherever our boldness has given us access to land and sea, we have established everlasting monuments of good *and wickedness*'). This 'boldness' of the noble races, expressed in mad, absurd, sudden ways, the incalculable, even the improbable aspect of their undertakings—Pericles emphasizes the *rhathymia** of the Athenians as a mark of distinction—their indifference and contempt for safety, life, limb, comfort, their horrific serenity and deep pleasure in all destruction, in the sensuality of victory and cruelty—all this is summarized for the victims in the image of the 'barbarian', of the 'evil enemy', of the 'Goth', the 'Vandal'. The deep, icy mistrust which the German arouses as soon as he comes to power, as he is doing now once again*—remains a throwback to that inextinguishable horror with which, for hundreds of years, Europe regarded the raging of the blond Germanic beast (although between the old Teutons and us modern Germans there scarcely exists a conceptual, let alone blood-, relationship). I once drew attention to Hesiod's embarrassment as he devised the succession of the ages of culture and sought to express them in terms of gold, silver, and bronze:* he knew of no other way to deal with the contradiction presented by the magnificent, but equally horrific and violent Homeric world than to divide this single age into two successive ones—the age of the heroes and demigods of Troy and Thebes,* as that world had survived in the memory of the noble races whose ancestors were to be found there; and then the bronze age, as that same age appeared to the descendants of the oppressed, dispossessed, badly treated, those who had been swept aside and bought: an age of bronze, as I said—hard, cold, cruel, without feeling and conscience, crushing everything and daubing everything with blood. Assuming that what is now in any case believed to be the 'truth' were true—that it is the *meaning of all culture* to breed a tame and civilized animal, a *domestic animal*, from the predatory animal 'man'—then there is no doubt that one would have to consider all the instincts of reaction and *ressentiment*, with whose help the noble races and their ideals were finally ruined and overcome, as the real *instruments of culture*. Which is not to say that those who possess these instincts are at the same time representatives of culture itself. Rather, the opposite is not only probable—no! today it is *patently obvious*! Those who possess the oppressive and vindictive instincts, the descendants of all European and non-European slavery, of all pre-Aryan population in particular—they represent the *regression* of humanity! These supposed 'instruments of culture' are a disgrace to mankind, they arouse suspicion and actually constitute an argument against 'culture' as a whole! One may have every right to remain fearful and suspicious of the blond beast beneath all noble races: but who would not a hundred times prefer fear accompanied by the possibility of admiration to *freedom* from fear accompanied by the disgusting sight of the failed, atrophied, and poisoned? And is this not *our* fate? What causes *our* revulsion from 'man' today?—for we *suffer* from man, there is no doubt.—*Not* fear; but rather the fact that we no longer have anything to fear from man; that 'man' squirms like a worm before us; that the 'tame man', the irremediably mediocre and unedifying man has already learnt to regard himself as goal and destination, as the meaning of history, as the 'higher man'—and even that he has a certain right to regard himself as such, in so far as he senses his superiority over the surplus of failed, sickly, tired, worn-out people who are beginning to make Europe smell, in so far as he represents something which remains at least relatively successful, something which is still capable of life, something which affirms life...

12

—At this point I cannot suppress a sigh and one remaining hope. What, of all things, am I unable to tolerate? The only thing which I find it impossible to deal with, which makes me choke and languish? Bad air! Bad air! When something failed draws near; when I am obliged to smell the entrails of a failed soul!... In comparison, what need, deprivation, bad weather, shallowness, toil, isolation cannot be borne? Basically, one can deal with everything else, born as one is to a subterranean existence of struggle; again and again one will reach the light, again and again experience the golden hour of victory—and then stand forth new-born, indestructible, tensed in readiness for what is new, more difficult, more distant, like a bow which every necessity merely draws tighter.—But from time to time let me be granted—if such things as divine patronesses actually exist beyond good and evil*—let me be granted a glimpse, just *one* glimpse of something complete, wholly successful, happy, powerful, triumphant, something still capable of inspiring fear! A glimpse of a man who justifies *mankind*, of a compensatory, redeeming stroke of luck on the part of man, a reason to retain *faith in mankind*!... For this is how things stand: the withering and levelling of European man constitutes *our* greatest danger, because it is a wearying sight... Today we see nothing with any desire to become greater, we sense that everything is going increasingly downhill, downhill, thinning out, getting more good-natured, cleverer, more comfortable, more mediocre, more indifferent, more Chinese, more Christian—man, there is no doubt, is 'improving' all the time... This and nothing else is the fate of Europe—along with our fear of man we have also forfeited our love, respect, and hope for him, even the will to him. The sight of man is now a wearying sight—what is nihilism today, if not *this*?... We are weary of *man*...

13

—But let us return to our problem: for our discussion of the problem of the *other* origin of 'good', of good as conceived by the man of *ressentiment*, requires its conclusion.—That lambs bear ill-will towards large birds of prey is hardly strange: but is in itself no reason to blame large birds of prey for making off with little lambs. And if the lambs say among themselves: 'These birds of prey are evil; and whoever is as little of a bird of prey as possible, indeed, rather the opposite, a lamb—should he not be said to be good?', then there can be no objection to setting up an ideal like this, even if the birds of prey might look down on it a little contemptuously and perhaps say to themselves: '*We* bear them no ill-will at all, these good lambs—indeed, we love them: there is nothing tastier than a tender lamb.' To demand of strength that it should *not* express itself as strength, that it should *not* be a will to overcome, overthrow, dominate, a thirst for enemies and resistance and triumph, makes as little sense as to demand of weakness that it should express itself as strength. A quantum of force is also a quantum of drive, will, action—in fact, it is nothing more than this driving, willing, acting, and it is only through the seduction of language (and through the fundamental errors of reason petrified in it)—language which understands and misunderstands all action as conditioned by an actor, by a 'subject'*—that it can appear otherwise. Just as the common people distinguish lightning from the flash of light and takes the latter as *doing*, as the effect of a subject which is called lightning, just so popular morality distinguishes strength from expressions of strength, as if behind the strong individual there were an indifferent substratum which was at *liberty* to express or not to express strength. But no such substratum exists; there is no 'being' behind doing, acting, becoming; 'the doer' is merely a fiction imposed on the doing—the doing itself is everything. Basically, the common people represent the doing twice over, when they make lightning flash—that is a doing doubled by another doing: it posits the same event once as cause and then once again as effect. The natural scientists do not fare any better when they say: 'Force moves, force causes', and the like—in spite of all its coldness, its freedom from emotion, our entire science is still subject to the seduction of language and has not shaken itself free of the monstrous changelings, the 'subjects', foisted upon it (the atom* is an example of such a changeling, as is the Kantian 'thing in itself'*). No wonder that the downtrodden and surreptitiously smouldering emotions of revenge and hatred exploit this belief in their own interests and maintain no belief with greater intensity than that *the strong may freely choose* to be weak, and the bird of prey to be lamb—and so they win the right to blame the bird of prey for simply being a bird of prey... If, out of the vindictive cunning of impotence, the oppressed, downtrodden, and violated tell themselves: 'Let us be different from the evil, that is, good! And the good man is the one who refrains from violation, who harms no one, who attacks no one, who fails to retaliate, who leaves revenge to God, who lives as we do in seclusion, who avoids all evil and above all asks little of life, as we do, the patient, the humble, the just.' When listened to coldly and without prejudice, this actually means nothing more than: 'We weak men are, after all, weak; it would be good if we refrained from doing anything *for which we lack sufficient strength.*' But this dry matter-of-factness, this cleverness of the lowest rank, which even insects possess (insects which, in situations of great danger, probably play dead in order not to do 'too much'), has, thanks to the forgery and self-deception of impotence, clothed itself in the magnificence of self-abnegating, calm, and patient virtue, exactly as if the weakness of the weak man itself—that is, his *essence*, his action, his whole single, unavoidable, irredeemable reality—were a free achievement, something willed, chosen, a *deed*, a *merit*. *Bound* to do so by his instinct of self-preservation and self-affirmation, an instinct which habitually sanctifies every lie, this kind of man discovered his faith in the indifferent, freely choosing 'subject'. The subject (or, to adopt a more popular idiom, the *soul*) has, therefore, been perhaps the best article of faith on earth so far, since it enables the majority of mortals, the weak and downtrodden of all sorts, to practise that sublime self-deception—the interpretation of weakness itself as freedom, of the way they simply are, as *merit*.

14

—Would anyone care to take a look into the secret depths of how *ideals are fabricated* on earth? Who is brave enough?... Very well! Here you can have an unobstructed view into this dark workshop. Wait just another moment, my dear Mr Daredevil Curiosity: your eyes must first get used to this false shimmering light... There! All right! Now tell us! What is going on down there? Describe what you see, man of the most dangerous curiosity—now it is *my* turn to listen.—

— 'I can see nothing, but hear all the more. There is a cautious, sly, soft mumbling and whispering coming from all corners. It seems to me that lies are being told; a sugary sweetness clings to every sound. Weakness is to be transformed into a *merit* through lies, there is no doubt—it is just as you said.'—

—Go on!

—'And the impotent failure to retaliate is to be transformed into "goodness"; craven fear into "humility"; submission to those one hates into "obedience" (obedience, that is, towards the authority who, so they claim, ordered this submission—they call him God). The inoffensive appearance of the weak man, even the cowardice which he possesses in abundance, his hesitation on the threshold, the inevitability of his being made to wait—all assume a good name here, as "patience", that is, as virtue *as such*; the inability to take revenge is called the refusal to take revenge, perhaps even forgiveness ("for *they* know not what they do*—we alone know what *they* do!"). There is also talk of "loving one's enemies"—accompanied by much perspiration.'

—Go on!

—'There is no doubt that they are miserable, all these mumbling forgers sitting in their corners, in spite of the fact that they huddle together for warmth—but they tell me that their misery is an election and a distinction conferred by God—one beats the dogs one loves the most; perhaps this misery is also a preparation, a test, a schooling, perhaps it is even more—something which will eventually be measured out and paid off at huge interest in gold, no! in happiness. That is what they call "salvation".'

—Go on!

—'Now they give me to understand that they are not only better than the powerful, the masters of the earth, whose spittle they are obliged to lick (*not* from fear, absolutely not! but because God commands respect for all authority)—that they are not only better, but also "have it better", or will "have it better" one day. But enough! enough! I can stand it no longer. Bad air! Bad air! This workshop where ideals are fabricated—it seems to me to stink of nothing but lies.'

—No! A moment longer! As yet you have said nothing about the masterpiece wrought by these experts in black magic who turn every dark shade into the white of milk and innocence—have you failed to notice their most perfect refinement, their boldest, finest, most intelligent, most duplicitous artistic stroke? Pay attention! These cellar-animals full of revenge and hatred—what exactly do they make out of revenge and hatred? Did you ever hear those particular words? Would you suspect, if you trusted to their words, that you were among men of *ressentiment*?...

—'I understand, I will keep my ears open (oh! oh! oh! and my nose *shut*). Only now do I hear what they have already repeated so often: "We good men—*we are the just*."—They do not call what they demand retaliation, but "the triumph of justice"; they do not hate their enemy, no! they hate "*injustice*", "godlessness"; their belief and hope is not the hope of revenge, the intoxication of sweet revenge (—"sweeter than honey" as Homer described it, already in his day), but the triumph of God, of the just God over the godless; what remains on earth for them to love is not their brothers in hatred, but their "brothers in love", as they say, all the good and just men on earth.'

—And what do they call the hope which serves to console them for all the suffering of life—their phantasmagoria of anticipated future salvation?

—'What? Am I hearing this right? They call it "the Last Judgement", the coming of *their* kingdom, the "Kingdom of God"—but *meanwhile* they live "in faith", "in love", "in hope".'

—Enough! Enough!

15

Faith in what? Love of what? Hope for what?—These weak men—for at the same time *they* too want to be strong, there is no doubt, at some time *their* 'kingdom' should also come—they call it simply 'the Kingdom of God', as I said: for one is so humble in all things! In order to experience it, one needs a long life, a life beyond death—eternal life, in fact, in order to take advantage for all eternity of the 'Kingdom of God' as compensation for this earthly life 'in faith, in love, in hope'. Compensation for what? Through what?... It seems to me that Dante made a vulgar error when, with fearful ingenuity, he set this inscription over the gates of Hell: 'I too was wrought by eternal love.'* In any case, the following would make a more appropriate inscription for the gate to the Christian Paradise: 'I too was wrought by eternal *hatred*'—assuming that a truth may stand over the gate to a lie! For what constitutes this Heaven's bliss?... We could probably guess by this stage; but it is better that in such things an authority who is not to be underestimated should expressly bear witness before us—Thomas Aquinas,* the great teacher and saint: *'Beati in regno coelesti videbunt poenas damnatorum*, **ut beatitudo illis magis complaceat**',* he says as meekly as a lamb. Or would one rather hear it in stronger terms, say, from the mouth of a triumphant Church Father* who advises his Christians against the cruel sensuality of public spectacles—and the reason? 'For faith offers us much more', he says, *De Spectac.* chapters 29 ff. [sic, actually 30], 'and something much stronger; thanks to redemption, completely different pleasures are available to us; in the place of athletes, we have our martyrs; if we want blood, then we have the blood of Christ... But what awaits us on the day of his return, his triumph!'—and then he continues, this delighted visionary:* '*At enim supersunt alia spectacula, ille ultimus et perpetuus judicii dies, ille nationibus insperatus, ille derisus, cum tanta saeculi vetustas et tot ejus nativitates uno igno haurientur. Quae tunc spectaculi latitudo!* **Quid admirer! Quid rideam! Ubi gaudeam! Ubi exultem**, *spectans tot et tantos* **reges**, *qui in coelum recepti nuntiabantur, cum ipso Jove et ipsis suis testibus in imis tenebris congemescentes! Item praesides* (the provincial office-holders) *persecutores dominici nominis saevioribus quam ipsi flammis saevierunt insultantibus contra Christianos liquescentes! Quos praeterea sapientes illos philosophos coram discipulis suis una conflagrantibus erubescentes, quibus nihil ad deum pertinere suadebant, quibus animas aut nullas aut non in pristina corpora redituras affirmabant! Etiam poëtas non ad Rhadamanti nec ad Minois,* sed ad inopinati Christi tribunal palpitantes! Tunc magis tragoedi audiendi, magis scilicet vocales* (in better voice, with even louder screams) *in sua propria calamitate; tunc histriones cognoscendi, solutiores multo per ignem; tunc spectandus auriga in flammea rota totus rubens, tunc xystici contemplandi non in gymnasiis, sed in igne jaculati, nisi quod ne tunc quidem illos velim vivos* [sic, *visos* in original], *ut qui malim ad eos potius conspectum* **insatiabilem** *conferre, qui in dominum desaevierunt. "Hic est ille", dicam, "fabri aut quaestuariae filius* (as all that follows and in particular this well-known designation of the mother of Jesus taken from the Talmud* indicates, Tertullian is from this point on referring to the Jews) *sabbati destructor, Samarites et daemonium habens. Hic est, quem a Juda redemistis, hic est ille arundine et colaphis diverberatus, sputamentis dedecoratus, felle et aceto potatus. Hic est, quem clam discentes subripuerunt, ut resurrexisse dicatur vel hortulanus detraxit, ne lactucae suae frequentia commeantium laederentur." Ut talia spectes,* **ut talibus exultes**, *quis tibi praetor aut consul aut quaestor aut sacerdos de sua liberalitate praestabit? Et tamen haec jam habemus quodammodo* **per fidem** *spiritu imaginante repraesentata. Ceterum qualia illa sunt, quae "nec oculus vidit nec auris audivit nec in cor hominis ascenderunt"?* (1 Corinthians 2: 9) *Credo circo et utraque cavea* (first and fourth rank or, according to others, comic and tragic theatre) *et omni stadio gratiora.'*—**Per fidem**:* so it is written.

16

Let us conclude. For thousands of years, a fearful struggle has raged on earth between the two opposed value-judgements, 'good and bad' and 'good and evil'; and as certain as it is that the second value-judgement has long been in the ascendant, there is even now no shortage of places where the outcome of the conflict remains undecided. It might even be said that the conflict has escalated in the interim and so become increasingly profound, more spiritual: so that today there is perhaps no more decisive mark of the '*higher nature*', of the more spiritual nature, than to be divided against oneself in this sense and to remain a battleground for these oppositions. The symbol for this struggle, written in a script which has remained legible throughout the whole of human history up until now, is called 'Rome against Judaea, Judaea against Rome'—so far, there has been no greater event than *this* struggle, *this* questioning, *this* mortal enmity and contradiction. Rome felt the Jew to be something like the incarnation of the unnatural, its monstrous opposite, as it were: in Rome, the Jew '*stood convicted* of hatred towards the whole of mankind':* rightly, in so far as one is entitled to associate the salvation and future of mankind with the absolute supremacy of the aristocratic values, the Roman values. How, on the other hand, did the Jews feel towards Rome? A thousand signs give us an indication; but it is sufficient to call to mind once more the Apocalypse according to St John, that most desolate of all the written outbursts which vindictiveness has on its conscience. (By the way, one should not underestimate the deep logic of the Christian instinct which inscribed this book of hatred with the name of the apostle of love, the one to whom it attributed that infatuated and enraptured gospel as his own—: there is a grain of truth in that, however much literary forgery may have been necessary to bring it about.*) The Romans were the strong and noble men, stronger and nobler than they had ever been on earth, or even dreamed themselves to be; every vestige left behind by them, every inscription is a delight, as long as one has an inkling of *what* is behind the writing. The Jews conversely were the priestly people of *ressentiment par excellence*, with an innate genius in matters of popular morality: one need only compare those peoples with related gifts, say, the Chinese or the Germans, with the Jews in order to appreciate the difference between first- and fifth-rate. Which of these is in the ascendant at the moment, Rome or Judaea? But there is no room for doubt: consider before whom one bows today in Rome as before the epitome of all the highest values—and not only in Rome, but over almost half the world, wherever man has been tamed or wants to be tamed—before *three Jews*, as one knows, and *one Jewess* (before Jesus of Nazareth, the fisherman Peter, the carpet-maker Paul, and the mother of the aforementioned Jesus, Mary). This is most remarkable: there is no doubt that Rome has been defeated. Admittedly, during the Renaissance there was a simultaneously glittering and sinister re-awakening of the classical ideal, of the noble mode of evaluation; beneath the weight of the new Judaicized Rome, which assumed the appearance of an ecumenical synagogue and called itself the 'Church', the old Rome itself moved like someone re-awakened from apparent death: but Judaea triumphed again immediately, thanks to a fundamentally plebeian (German and English) movement of *ressentiment*, known as the Reformation, as well as what necessarily arose from it, the restoration of the Church and the restoration also of the old, grave-like peace of classical Rome. In an even more decisive and profound sense than previously, Judaea triumphed once more over the classical ideal with the French Revolution: the last political nobility in Europe, that of *France* in the seventeenth and eighteenth centuries, collapsed under the instincts of popular *ressentiment*—never before had a greater celebration, a noisier excitement been heard on earth! Admittedly, the most monstrous and unexpected thing happened in the middle of all this: the ideal of the ancients itself emerged *in flesh and blood* and with unheard-of splendour before the eyes and conscience of mankind. Against the old deceitful slogan of *ressentiment*—the *prerogative of the greatest number*—against the will to the belittlement, humiliation, levelling, decline, and twilight of man, the fearful and delightful slogan of the *prerogative of the few* rang out once more, stronger, simpler, more insistent than ever! Like a last gesture in the *other* direction, Napoleon* appeared, the most individual and most belatedly born man ever to have existed, and in him the incarnation of the problem of the *noble ideal as such*—consider *what* a problem it is, Napoleon, this synthesis of the *inhuman* and the *superhuman*...

17

—Was that the end of it? Was that greatest of all ideal oppositions then placed *ad acta** for all time? Or only postponed, indefinitely postponed?... Will the old flame not inevitably flare up again at some time in an even more fearful way, after much lengthier preparation? Moreover, is this not the very thing which we should desire with all our strength? should even will? should even promote?... Anyone who, like my reader, starts to reflect at this point and to pursue his thoughts will find no early end to them—reason enough for me to come to an end, assuming that my *aim* has long since become sufficiently clear, the aim of that dangerous slogan written on the body of my last book: 'Beyond Good and Evil'... This at the very least does *not* mean 'Beyond Good and Bad'.— —

Note: I take the opportunity afforded by this essay to give public and formal expression to a wish which I have previously mooted only in occasional conversations with academics: that some philosophy faculty or another might render outstanding service to the promotion of the *historical* study of *morality* through offering a series of academic prizes—perhaps this book might serve to give a powerful impetus in this very direction. Should this possibility be pursued, the following question might be suggested: it merits the attention of philologists and historians as much as that of philosophers by profession—

'What indications for the direction of further research does linguistics, and in particular the study of etymology, provide for the history of the development of moral concepts?'

—On the other hand, it is admittedly just as necessary to secure the interest of physiologists and physicians in the exploration of this problem (of the *value* of previous evaluations): here too it might be left to the specialist philosophers to act as spokesmen and mediators in this matter, once they have largely succeeded in reshaping the original relationship of mutual aloofness and suspicion which obtains between the disciplines of philosophy, physiology, and medicine into the most amicable and fruitful exchange. In fact, all tables of commandments, all 'Thou shalts' known to history or ethnological research, certainly require *physiological* investigation and interpretation* prior to psychological examination. Equally, all await a critique from the medical sciences. The question: what is the *value* of this or that table of commandments and 'morality'? should be examined from the most varied perspectives; in particular, the question of its value *to what end?* cannot be examined too closely. For example, something possessing clear value for the greatest possible survival capacity of a race (or for increasing its powers of adaptation to a certain climate or for the preservation of the greatest number) would not have anything like the same value if what was at issue were the development of a stronger type. The welfare of the greatest number and the welfare of the few represent opposed points of view on value: to hold the former as of intrinsically higher value may be left to the naïveté of English biologists... From now on, *all* disciplines have to prepare the future task of the philosopher: this task being understood as the solution of the *problem of value*, the determination of the *hierarchy of values*.—

SECOND ESSAY

'Guilt', 'Bad Conscience', and Related Matters

1

The breeding of an animal which is *entitled to make promises*—is this not the paradoxical task which nature has set itself with respect to man? Is this not the real problem which man not only poses but faces also?... The extent to which this problem has been solved must seem all the more surprising to someone who fully appreciates the countervailing force of *forgetfulness*. Forgetfulness is no mere *vis inertiae*,* as the superficial believe; it is rather an active—in the strictest sense, positive—inhibiting capacity, responsible for the fact that what we absorb through experience impinges as little on our consciousness during its digestion (what might be called its 'psychic assimilation'*) as does the whole manifold process of our physical nourishment, that of so-called 'physical assimilation'. The temporary shutting of the doors and windows of consciousness; guaranteed freedom from disturbance by the noise and struggle caused by our underworld of obedient organs as they co-operate with and compete against one another; a little silence, a little *tabula rasa** of consciousness, making room for the new, making room above all for the superior functions and functionaries—those of governing, anticipating, planning ahead (since our organism is structured as an oligarchy)—such is the use of what I have called active forgetfulness, an active forgetfulness whose function resembles that of a concierge preserving mental order, calm, and decorum. On this basis, one may appreciate immediately to what extent there could be no happiness, no serenity, no hope, no pride, no *present* without forgetfulness. The man in whom this inhibiting apparatus is damaged and out of order may be compared to a dyspeptic (and not only compared)—he is never 'through' with anything... Even this necessarily forgetful animal—in whom forgetting is a strength, a form of *robust* health—has now bred for himself a counter-faculty, a memory, by means of which forgetfulness is in certain cases suspended—that is, those which involve promising. This development is not merely the result of a passive inability to rid oneself of an impression once etched on the mind, nor of the incapacity to digest a once-given word with which one is never through, but represents rather an active *will* not to let go, an ongoing willing of what was once willed, a real *memory of the will*: so that between the original 'I will', 'I shall do', and the actual realization of the will, its *enactment*, a world of new and strange things, circumstances, even other acts of will may safely intervene, without causing this long chain of the will to break. But how much all this presupposes! In order to dispose of the future in advance in this way, how much man must first have learnt to distinguish necessity from accident! To think in terms of causality, to see and anticipate from afar, to posit ends and means with certainty, to be able above all to reckon and calculate! For that to be the case, how much man himself must have become *calculable*, *regular*, *necessary*, even to his own mind, so that finally he would be able to vouch for himself *as future*, in the way that someone making a promise does!

2

Such is the long history of the origin of *responsibility*. As we have already grasped, the task of breeding an animal which is entitled to make promises presupposes as its condition a more immediate task, that of first *making* man to a certain extent necessary, uniform, an equal among equals, regular and consequently calculable. The enormous labour of what I have called the 'morality of custom'—the special work of man on himself throughout the longest era of the human race, his whole endeavour *prior to the onset of history*, all this finds its meaning, its great justification—regardless of the degree to which harshness, tyranny, apathy, and idiocy are intrinsic to it—in the following fact: it was by means of the morality of custom and the social strait-jacket that man was really *made* calculable. By way of contrast, let us place ourselves at the other end of this enormous process, at the point where the tree finally bears its fruit, where society and its morality of custom finally reveal the *end* to which they were merely a means: there we find as the ripest fruit on their tree the *sovereign individual*, the individual who resembles no one but himself, who has once again broken away from the morality of custom, the autonomous supra-moral individual (since 'autonomous' and 'moral' are mutually exclusive)—in short, the man with his own independent, enduring will, the man who is *entitled to make promises*. And in him we find a proud consciousness, tense in every muscle, of *what* has finally been achieved here, of what has become incarnate in him—a special consciousness of power and freedom, a feeling of the ultimate completion of man. This liberated man, who is really *entitled* to make promises, this master of *free* will, this sovereign—how should he not be aware of his superiority over everything which cannot promise and vouch for itself? How should he not be aware of how much trust, how much fear, how much respect he arouses—he '*deserves*' all three—and how much mastery over circumstances, over nature, and over all less reliable creatures with less enduring wills is necessarily given into his hands along with this self-mastery? The 'free' man—the owner of an enduring, indestructible will—possesses also in this property his *measure of value*: looking out at others from his own vantage-point, he bestows respect or contempt. Necessarily, he respects those who are like him—the strong and reliable (those who are *entitled* to make promises), that is, anyone who promises like a sovereign—seriously, seldom, slowly—who is sparing with his trust, who *confers distinction* when he trusts, who gives his word as something which can be relied on, because he knows himself strong enough to uphold it even against accidents, even 'against fate'. Even so, he will have to keep the toe of his boot poised for the cowering dogs who make promises without entitlement, and hold his stick at the ready for the liar who breaks his word the moment he utters it. The proud knowledge of this extraordinary privilege of *responsibility*, the consciousness of this rare freedom, this power over oneself and over fate has sunk down into his innermost depths and has become an instinct, a dominant instinct—what will he call it, this dominant instinct, assuming that he needs a name for it? About that there can be no doubt: this sovereign man calls it his *conscience*...

3

His conscience?... It may be surmised in advance that the concept of 'conscience'—which we meet here in its highest, almost disconcerting form—is the product of a long history and series of transformations. To be able to vouch for oneself, and to do so with pride, and so to have the *right to affirm oneself*—that is, as I have said, a ripe fruit, but also a *late* fruit. How long this fruit had to hang sharp and bitter on the tree! And for an even longer time there was no sign of such a fruit—no one would have had the right to promise it, in spite of the fact that this alone was the end towards which the entire preparation and growth of the tree was directed!—'How does one give the man-animal a memory? How does one impress something on this partly insensate, partly idiotic ephemeral understanding, this incarnated forgetfulness, so that it remains present to mind?'... As we might imagine, the means employed to find a solution or answer to this ancient problem have been far from tender; there is, perhaps, nothing more frightening and more sinister in the whole prehistory of man than his *technique for remembering things*. 'Something is branded in, so that it stays in the memory: only that which *hurts* incessantly is remembered'—this is a central proposition of the oldest (and unfortunately also the most enduring) psychology on earth. One may even be tempted to say that something of this horror—by means of which promises were once made all over the earth, and guarantees and undertakings given—something of this *survives* still wherever solemnity, seriousness, secrecy, and sombre colours are found in the life of men and nations: the past, the longest, deepest, harshest past, breathes on us and wells up in us, whenever we become 'serious'. Things never proceeded without blood, torture, and victims, when man thought it necessary to forge a memory for himself. The most horrifying sacrifices and offerings (including sacrifice of the first-born), the most repulsive mutilations (castrations, for example), the cruellest rituals of all religious cults (and all religions are at their deepest foundations systems of cruelty)—all these things originate from that instinct which guessed that the most powerful aid to memory was pain. In a certain sense, the whole of asceticism belongs here: a few ideas are to be made inextinguishable, omnipresent, unforgettable, 'fixed'—with the aim of hypnotizing the whole nervous system and intellect by means of these 'fixed ideas'—and the ascetic procedures and forms of life are the means of freeing these ideas from competition with all other ideas, in order to make them 'unforgettable'. The worse mankind's memory was, the more frightening its customs appear; the harshness of punishment codes, in particular, gives a measure of how much effort it required to triumph over forgetfulness and to make these ephemeral slaves of emotion and desire mindful of a few primitive requirements of social cohabitation. We Germans certainly do not regard ourselves as a particularly cruel and hard-hearted people, still less as particularly frivolous and inclined to live for the moment; but one need only look at our ancient penal codes to discover how much effort it cost to breed a 'people of thinkers' on this earth (I mean by that: *the* European people, among whom even today the maximum of trust, earnestness, lack of taste, and sobriety is still to be found, and which on the basis of these characteristics has a claim to rearing every kind of mandarin in Europe). In order to master the clumsiness and brutality of their basic plebeian instincts, these Germans have had recourse to frightening means in forging themselves a memory: one need only think of the old German punishments, of stoning, for example (—even in myth the millstone falls on the head of the guilty), breaking on the wheel (the most original invention and speciality of the German genius in the field of punishment!), impalement on the stake, tearing apart or trampling by horses ('quartering'), boiling the criminal in oil or wine (even in the fourteenth and fifteenth century), the popular practice of flaying ('leatherwork'), the excision of a pound of flesh from the torso; covering the criminal with honey and leaving him to the flies in the scorching sun. With the help of such images and procedures one eventually memorizes five or six 'I will not's, thus giving one's *promise* in return for the advantages offered by society. And indeed! with the help of this sort of memory, one eventually did come to 'see reason'!—Ah, reason, seriousness, mastery over the emotions, the whole murky affair which goes by the name of thought, all these privileges and showpieces of man: what a high price has been paid for them! how much blood and horror is at the bottom of all 'good things'!

4

But how then did that other 'murky affair', the sense of guilt, the whole matter of 'bad conscience', originate?—And here we return to our genealogists of morals. To repeat myself—or perhaps I have not yet said it at all?—they are of no use. A smattering of personal experience, limited merely to the 'modern'; no knowledge, no will to knowledge of the past; even less of a historical instinct, the 'second sight' which is the very thing required here—and in spite of all that, still to go about the business of the history of morality: this must rightly produce results whose relationship to the truth is a good deal less than tenuous. For example, have the previous exponents of the genealogy of morals had even the slightest inkling that the central moral concept of 'guilt' [*Schuld*] originated from the very material concept of 'debt' [*Schulden*]? Or that punishment as a form of repayment has developed in complete independence from any presupposition about free will or the lack of it?—This is true to such an extent that it was only after reaching an *advanced* stage of humanization that the animal 'man' could even begin to make the much more primitive distinctions between 'deliberate', 'negligent', 'arbitrary', 'of sound mind', and their opposites and apply them to the infliction of punishment. The thought which is nowadays so proper and apparently so natural, so unavoidable, the thought which had to serve as the explanation for how the sense of justice came to exist on earth at all—the thought that 'the criminal deserves punishment, because he could have acted otherwise'—is in fact an extremely recent and refined form of human judgement and logic; whoever displaces it on to the origins of human judgement is guilty of tampering crudely with the psychology of mankind in its early stages. Throughout the longest period of human history, punishment was not exacted *because* the trouble-maker was held responsible for his action, that is, it was *not* exacted on the assumption that only the guilty man was to be punished, but rather, just as nowadays parents still punish their children, out of anger at harm done, anger which is then taken out on the person who causes it—albeit held in check and modified by the idea that any damage somehow has an *equivalent* and really can be paid off, even if this is through the *pain* of the culprit. Where has this ancient, deeply rooted, and by now perhaps ineradicable idea, this idea of the equivalence between damage and pain, drawn its strength from? I have already given it away: from the contractual relationship between *creditor* and *debtor*, which is as old as the concept of 'legal subjects' itself and which points back in turn to the fundamental forms of buying, selling, exchange, wheeling and dealing.

5

As might be expected from what I have said before, when we consider these contractual relations there is no doubt that the mankind of an earlier age which created or sanctioned them arouses a degree of suspicion and revulsion on our part. For this is where *promises* are made; at issue here is the *making* of a memory for the man who promises; this is where, so one may suspect, hard, cruel, and painful things will be found. In order to instil trust for his promise of repayment, in order to give a guarantee for the seriousness and sacredness of his promise, in order to impress repayment as a duty and obligation sharply upon his own conscience, the debtor contractually pledges to the creditor in the event of non-payment something which he otherwise still 'possesses', something over which he still has power—for example, his body or his wife or his freedom or even his life (or, under certain religious conditions, even his salvation, the good of his soul, ultimately even the peace of his grave: as in Egypt, where even in the grave the corpse of the debtor finds no respite from the creditor—and among the Egyptians this peace meant a great deal). In particular, however, the creditor could subject the body of the debtor to all sorts of humiliation and torture—he could, for example, excise as much flesh as seemed commensurate with the size of the debt. For this purpose, there have existed from the earliest times precise and in part horrifically detailed measurements, *legal* measurements, of the individual limbs and parts of the body. I take it as already a sign of progress, as proof of a freer, *more Roman* conception of law, one grander in its calculations, that the twelve-table legislation of Rome* decreed the amount which creditors excised in such cases a matter of indifference, '*si plus minusve secuerunt, ne fraude esto*'.* Let us be clear about the logic of this whole form of exchange: it is alien enough. The equivalence is established by the fact that, instead of a direct compensation for the damage done (i.e. instead of money, land, possessions of whatever sort), a sort of *pleasure* is conceded to the creditor as a form of repayment and recompense—the pleasure of being able to vent his power without a second thought on someone who is powerless, the enjoyment '*de faire le mal pour le plaisir de le faire*',* the pleasure of violation. This enjoyment will be prized all the more highly, the lower the creditor stands in the social order, and can easily appear to him as the choicest morsel, even as a foretaste of a higher rank. By means of the 'punishment' inflicted on the debtor, the creditor partakes of a *privilege of the masters*: at last, he too has the opportunity to experience the uplifting feeling of being entitled to despise and mistreat someone as 'beneath him'—or at least, in cases where the actual power and execution of punishment has already passed to the 'authorities', to *see* this person despised and mistreated. So this compensation consists in an entitlement and right to cruelty.—

6

It is in *this* sphere, in legal obligations, then, that the moral conceptual world of 'guilt', 'conscience', 'duty', 'sacred duty' originates—its beginning, like the beginning of everything great on earth, has long been steeped in blood. And might one not add that the world has basically never since shaken off a certain odour of blood and torture? (not even with old Kant:

the categorical imperative gives off a whiff of cruelty...). Likewise, this is where the sinister and by now perhaps inextricable entanglement of the ideas 'guilt and pain' was first woven together. To repeat the question: to what extent can suffering compensate for 'debt'? To the extent that *inflicting* pain occasions the greatest pleasure, to the extent that the injured party exchanges for the damage done, together with the displeasure it causes, an extraordinary pleasure which offsets it: the opportunity to *inflict* suffering—an actual *festivity*, something which, as I said, is valued all the more highly the more it contradicts the social standing of the creditor. This is said by way of a hypothesis: for it is difficult to see to the bottom of such subterranean things, quite apart from the fact that it is unpleasant; and anyone who is clumsy and hasty enough to introduce the concept of revenge at this point, has concealed and obscured his view rather than made it clearer (—for revenge itself leads back to the same problem: 'How can inflicting pain provide satisfaction?'). It appears to me that the delicacy, even more the hypocrisy of tame domestic animals (by this, I mean modern man, I mean us) is loath to envisage to what extent *cruelty* constituted the great festivity and pleasure of mankind in earlier days, and was even an ingredient in almost all of its pleasures. On the other hand, how naïvely, how innocently their need for cruelty emerges, how as a matter of principle they posit this very 'disinterested malice' (or, to use Spinoza's formula, *sympathia malevolens**) as a *normal* characteristic of mankind—: and in the process posit it as something to which the conscience heartily *assents*! Perhaps even today a more perceptive eye would discern enough of this earliest and most fundamental human festivity and joy: in *Beyond Good and Evil*, §229 (and even in *Daybreak*, §§18, 77, 113) I took care to point out the transformation of cruelty into something ever more spiritual and 'divine',* a process which runs through the whole history of higher culture (and, in a significant sense, even constitutes it). In any case, even in relatively recent times princely weddings and popular festivities in a grand style were inconceivable without executions, torture, or perhaps even an *auto-da-fé*.* Similarly, it was impossible to conceive of a noble household without a creature upon whom one could vent one's malice and cruel teasing without a second thought (—remember, for example, Don Quixote at the court of the Duchess:* today we read the whole *Don Quixote* with a bitter taste in our mouths, almost with a sense of torture, and so would seem very alien, very inscrutable to its author and his contemporaries—they read it with the best of all consciences as the most cheerful of books, they almost laughed themselves to death over it). To witness suffering does one good, to inflict it even more so—that is a harsh proposition, but a fundamental one, an old, powerful, human all-too-human proposition, one to which perhaps even the apes would subscribe: it is said that in devising bizarre cruelties they already to a large extent anticipate and at the same time 'rehearse' man. No festivity without cruelty: such is the lesson of the earliest, longest period in the history of mankind—and even in punishment there is so much that is *festive*!

7

—By the way, these thoughts are not at all intended as grist to the mill of pessimistic disgust with life as it grinds tunelessly on. On the contrary, I shall expressly testify that in the days before mankind grew ashamed of its cruelty, before pessimists existed, life on earth was more cheerful than it is now. The darkness of the sky over man has always deepened in proportion to the growth of the shame of man *before man*. The tired, pessimistic view, the mistrust of the enigma of life, the icy No of disgust at life—these are not the characteristics of the *most evil* period of mankind: rather, they emerge as the swamp-weeds they are only once the quagmire to which they belong is already in existence—I mean the sickly softening and moralizing by means of which the animal 'man' finally learns to feel ashamed of all his instincts. On his way to becoming an 'angel' (in order to avoid using a harsher word here), man has bred for himself that dyspepsia and furred tongue, as a result of which not only the joy and innocence of the animal have become repugnant to him, but even life itself has lost its savour—so that man pinches his nose as he examines himself, and along with Pope Innocent III* disapprovingly draws up an inventory of his repulsive characteristics ('unclean conception, disgusting form of nourishment in the mother's body, base quality of the material from which man develops, appalling stench, secretion of saliva, urine, vomit'). Nowadays, when suffering is always summoned as the foremost argument *against* existence, as its worst question-mark, we would do well to remember the times when exactly the opposite conclusion was drawn, because mankind did not want to forgo the *infliction* of suffering, seeing in it an enchantment of the first rank, an actual seduction and lure *in favour of* life. By way of consolation to the more delicate, perhaps in those days pain did not hurt us as much as it does today. At least, that might be the conclusion of a physician who has treated Negroes* (these taken as representatives of prehistoric man—) for serious cases of internal inflammation; such inflammation would bring even the best organized European to the brink of despair—but this is *not* the case with Negroes. (The curve of human capacity for pain seems in fact to fall off extraordinarily abruptly, once past the upper ten thousand or ten million of the higher culture; and I personally have no doubt that in comparison with a *single* painful night undergone by one hysterical little bluestocking, the total suffering of all the animals put to the knife in the interests of scientific research simply does not enter into consideration.) Perhaps the possibility might even be entertained that pleasure in cruelty need not actually have died out: considering the extent to which pain hurts more nowadays, all that it had to do was sublimate and refine itself*—that is, it had to appear translated into the imagination and the psyche, embellished only with such harmless names as were incapable of arousing the suspicion of even the most delicate hypocritical conscience ('tragic sympathy' is such a name; another is '*les nostalgies de la croix*'*). The aspect of suffering which actually causes outrage is not suffering itself, but the meaninglessness of suffering: but neither for the Christian who has interpreted a whole secret machinery of salvation into suffering, nor for the naïve man of earlier times, who knew how to interpret all suffering in relation to those who actually inflict it or view it as a spectacle, did such a *meaningless* suffering actually exist. So that hidden, undiscovered, and unwitnessed suffering could be banished from the world and honestly negated, mankind was at that time virtually forced to invent gods and supernatural beings of all heights and depths—in short, to invent something which can penetrate secrets, see in the dark, and would only with great reluctance pass up an interesting spectacle of pain. With the help of such inventions, life at that time demonstrated its expertise in the trick for which it has always shown an aptitude—that is, self-justification, justifying its 'evil'. Nowadays perhaps, it needs to that end the assistance of other inventions (the notion of life as enigma, of life as epistemological problem, for example). 'Every evil is justified, whose sight uplifts a god': so ran the prehistoric logic of feeling—and really, did this apply to prehistory alone? The gods envisaged as friends of *cruel* spectacles—oh how far this ancient idea extends even into our human development in Europe! One need only consult Calvin and Luther* on this matter. In any case, it is certain that even the *Greeks* knew no more pleasant seasoning for the happiness of the gods than the joys of cruelty. With what eyes, then, do you think Homer let his gods gaze down upon the fates of men? What ultimate meaning did Trojan Wars and similar fearful tragedies have? There is absolutely no doubt about it: they were intended as *festive theatre* for the gods: and in so far as the poet is more 'divinely' constituted than the rest of men, probably as festive theatre for the poets too... And in the very same way the later moral philosophers of Greece thought the eyes of god still gazed down on the moral turmoil, the heroism and self-torture of the virtuous man: the 'Hercules of duty'* was on stage, and he knew it; unwitnessed virtue was for this people of actors something completely unthinkable. That so daring, so disastrous invention of the philosophers, first devised for Europe at that time—the invention of 'free will', the absolute spontaneity of man in good and evil—should it not have been devised primarily in order to assure people that the interest of the gods in men, in human virtue, could *never be exhausted*? On this stage-world, real novelty, really unprecedented suspense, plot-complications and catastrophes ought never to be in short supply: an absolutely deterministic world might be anticipated in advance and so quickly become tiresome for the gods—

reason enough for these *friends of the gods*, the philosophers, not to expect the gods to put up with such a deterministic world! In the whole of the ancient world—an essentially public, essentially visible world, which could not conceive of happiness without theatre and festivals—mankind is full of delicate consideration for 'the spectators'.—And, as I said before, even in great *punishment* there is so much that is festive!...

8

To take up once again the trail of our investigation, the feeling of guilt, of personal responsibility originated, as we have seen, in the earliest and most primordial relationship between men, in the relationship between buyer and seller, debtor and creditor: it is here that one man first encountered another, here that one man first *measured himself* against another. No level of civilization, however rudimentary, has been found where something of this relationship cannot be discerned. Setting prices, estimating values, devising equivalents, making exchanges—this has preoccupied the very earliest thinking of man to such an extent that it, in a certain sense, constitutes *thinking as such*: it is here that the earliest form of astuteness was bred, here likewise, we might suppose, that human pride, man's feeling of superiority over other animals originated. Perhaps our word 'man' (*manas**) still reveals something of *this* very perception of the self: man designated himself as the being who estimates values, who evaluates and measures, as *the* 'measuring animal'. Buying and selling, together with the psychology which accompanies them, are older than even the beginnings of any social form of organization and association. It was from the most rudimentary form of personal law that the budding sense of exchange, contract, debt, law, obligation, compensation first *translated* itself into the crudest and earliest social complexes (in their relation to similar complexes), along with the habit of comparing, measuring, and calculating power in relation to power. The eye was now adjusted to this perspective: and with that clumsy consistency which is peculiar to the thinking of mankind in earlier times, a thinking which is slow to get under way, but which once in motion continues relentlessly in the same direction, one soon arrives at the great generalization: 'Everything has its price; *everything* can be paid off'—the earliest and most naïve canon of moral *justice*, the beginning of all 'neighbourliness', all 'fairness', all 'good will', all 'objectivity' on earth. Justice at the earliest stage of its development is the good will which prevails among those of roughly equal power to come to terms with one another, to 'come to an understanding' once more through a settlement—and to *force* those who are less powerful to agree a settlement among themselves.—

9

To retain still the criteria of prehistory (which, moreover, either persists into the present or remains a possibility at all times): the community stands in the same important fundamental relationship to its members as the creditor does to his debtors. One lives in a community, one enjoys the advantages of a community (oh what advantages! we sometimes underestimate them today), one lives protected, looked after, in peace and trust, without a care for certain forms of harm and hostility to which the man *outside*, the 'outlaw' is exposed—a German understands what *'Elend'*, *êlend** meant originally—, since man has pledged and committed himself to the community as regards this harm and hostility. What will happen *if the pledge is broken*? The community, the deceived creditor, will see that it receives payment, in so far as it can, one may count on that. The direct harm caused is the least matter of concern here: leaving that aside, the criminal is above all someone who 'breaks', someone who breaks a contractual commitment, breaks his word* *towards the whole community*, in relation to all the goods and amenities of communal life in which he previously shared. The criminal is a debtor who not only fails to repay the advantages and advances offered to him but even attacks his creditors, and for that reason he is from that point on not only, as is just, denied all these goods and advantages—he is also reminded of *what these goods represent*. The fury of the aggrieved creditor, of the community, returns him to the wild and outlaw status from which he was previously protected: it expels him—and now every kind of hostility may be vented on him. On this level of morality, 'punishment' is simply the image, the *mimus** of normal behaviour towards a hated enemy, who lies prostrate and defenceless, bereft not only of every right and protection, but also of all hope of grace. Punishment is, then, the prerogative of the victor and celebration of the *Vae victis!** in all its ruthlessness and cruelty—which explains how war itself (including the warlike cult of sacrifice) has produced all the *forms* in which punishment appears throughout history.

10

As its power increases, a community no longer takes the misdemeanours of the individual so seriously, because they no longer seem to pose the same revolutionary threat to the existence of the whole as they did previously: the evil-doer is no longer 'outlawed' and expelled, universal fury is no longer given the same permission to vent itself on him without restraint. Rather, from now on the whole community will take care to defend and protect the evil-doer from this fury, and particularly from the fury of the directly injured party. Compromise with the fury of the man immediately affected by the misdeed; an effort to localize the case and to obviate further or even general participation and unrest; attempts to find equivalents and to settle the whole business (the *compositio**); above all, the increasingly definite emergence of the will to accept every crime as in some sense capable of being *paid off*, and so, at least to a certain extent, to *isolate* the criminal from his deed—these are the characteristics which become more and more clearly stamped on the later development of the penal code. As the power and self-confidence of a community grows, so its penal legislation is always relaxed; each weakening and deeper endangering of the community brings the return of harsher forms. The humanity of the 'creditor' has always increased in proportion to his wealth; ultimately, the *measure* of his wealth becomes how much harm he can sustain without suffering. It is not impossible to conceive of a society whose *consciousness of power* would allow it the most refined luxury there is—that of allowing those who do it harm to go *unpunished*. 'Of what concern are these parasites to me?', it would be entitled to say. 'May they live and prosper: I am strong enough to allow that!'... The justice which began with: 'Everything can be paid off, everything must be paid off', ends with a look the other way as those who are unable to pay are allowed to run free—it ends as every good thing on earth ends, by *cancelling itself out*. This self-cancellation* of justice: the beautiful name it goes by is well enough known—*grace*; needless to say, it remains the prerogative of the most powerful man, even better, his domain beyond the law.

11

—Let me say a word here by way of refutation of recent attempts to seek the origin of justice on a completely different ground—that is, in *ressentiment*. And let me first whisper something in the ear of the psychologists, just in case they might for once want to study *ressentiment* at close quarters: this plant now blooms most beautifully among anarchists and anti-Semites,* in hidden places, just where it has always flowered, like the violet, although its perfume is admittedly somewhat different. And as like must always proceed from like, so it will come as no surprise to learn that it is from these very same circles that attempts to sanctify *revenge* under the name of *justice* emanate, just as they have so often in the past—compare I §14 above—, as if justice were at bottom merely an extension of the feeling of injury—and with revenge to bring all the *reactive* feelings retroactively* to a position of honour. I myself would be the last to take offence at this latter development: with respect to the whole biological problem (in relation to which the value of those feelings has previously been underestimated) this would seem to me a *merit*. The only point to which I would draw attention is that it is from the spirit of *ressentiment* itself that this new nuance of scientific fairness grows (to the advantage of hatred, envy, resentment, rancour, revenge). For this 'scientific fairness' is immediately abdicated, leaving room for accents of mortal enmity and prejudice, as soon as another group of feelings come under scrutiny, a group of feelings which, it seems to me, are of a much greater biological value than the reactive feelings and as a consequence rightly deserve to be evaluated and appreciated in a *scientific* manner: that is, the really *active* feelings, such as the desire to dominate, to possess, and the like. (E. Dühring*, *The Value of Life*; *The Course of Philosophy*; basically throughout his work). So much said against this tendency in general: but as for Dühring's single proposition that the home of justice is to be sought on the ground of reactive feeling, the interests of truth require a blunt response in the form of this alternative proposition: the ground of reactive feeling is the *last* ground occupied by the spirit of justice! If it really is the case that the just man remains just even in his dealings with those who do him harm (and not merely cold, measured, foreign, indifferent: being just is always a *positive* mode of behaviour), if the high, clear, objective vision of the just, the *judging* eye, as penetrating as it is mild, is not obscured even under the onslaught of personal injury, humiliation, and suspicion, then that is a piece of perfection and the highest mastery on earth—something which one would not in all wisdom expect to find here, and in which one should not too readily *believe*. There is no doubt that on average just a tiny amount of aggression, malice, and insinuation is sufficient to make even the most honest people see red and to deprive them of an impartial eye. The active, attacking, encroaching man is still a hundred paces closer to justice than his reactive counterpart; to the extent that he has no need to evaluate his object in a false and prejudiced manner as the reactive man does. For this reason, in fact, the aggressive man, the stronger, braver, nobler man has at all times had the *freer* eye, the *better* conscience on his side. Conversely, perhaps it is clear by now on whose conscience the invention of 'bad conscience' rests—that of the man of *ressentiment*! As a final point, one need only consult history: where has the entire administration of law, and also the actual need for law, made its home up to now? In the sphere of the reactive men? Not at all: rather in that of the active, the strong, the spontaneous, the aggressive man. From a historical point of view—let it be said to the annoyance of the aforementioned agitator* (who once made the following admission about himself: 'The doctrine of revenge runs through all my works and efforts like the red thread of justice')—the law represents rather the struggle *against* the reactive feelings, the war against these feelings in the interests of the active and aggressive forces, which use their strength in part to contain and moderate the extravagance of reactive pathos and to compel a settlement. Wherever justice is practised, wherever justice is upheld, one sees a stronger power seek means to put an end to the senseless raging of *ressentiment* among weaker powers subordinate to it (whether groups or individuals). This is achieved partly by removing the object of *ressentiment* from their hands, partly by substituting for their revenge the struggle against the enemies of peace and order, partly by inventing, suggesting, and under certain circumstances imposing settlements, partly by elevating to a norm certain equivalents for damage done, to which from now on and for all time *ressentiment* is referred. But the most decisive action which the highest power takes and implements against the predominance of reactive and retroactive feelings*—and this is the action it always undertakes, as soon as it is somehow strong enough to do so—, is the establishment of the law, the imperious explanation of what in its eyes passes as permitted, as right, and what as forbidden, as wrong. And once the law is established, by treating encroachments and arbitrary acts on the part of individuals or whole groups as a heinous crime against the law, as rebellion against itself, the highest power diverts the feeling of its subordinates from the most immediate harm caused by such crime until by this route it eventually reaches the opposite goal to that desired by all revenge, which only sees and admits as valid the point of view of the injured party. From now on, the eye is trained for an increasingly *impersonal* evaluation of the deed, and this includes even the eye of the injured party himself (albeit last of all, as was previously noted).—Accordingly, 'right' and 'wrong' exist only from the moment the law is established (and *not*, as Dühring would have it, from the moment of injury). To talk of right and wrong *as such* is senseless; *in themselves*, injury, violation, exploitation, destruction can of course be nothing 'wrong', in so far as life operates *essentially*—that is, in terms of its basic functions—through injury, violation, exploitation, and destruction, and cannot be conceived in any other way. One is forced to admit something even more disturbing: that, from the highest biological point of view, legal conditions may be nothing more than *exceptional states of emergency*, partial restrictions which the will to life in its quest for power provisionally imposes on itself in order to serve its overall goal: the creation of *larger* units of power. A state of law conceived as sovereign and general, not as a means in the struggle between power-complexes, but as a means *against* struggle itself, in the manner of Dühring's communist cliché according to which each will must recognize every other will as equal, would be a principle *hostile to life*, would represent the destruction and dissolution of man, an attack on the future of man, a sign of exhaustion, a secret path towards nothingness.—

12

At this point, let me add another word on the origin and aim of punishment—two problems which are, or at least ought to be, clearly distinguished, but are, unfortunately, more usually conflated. How, then, do the genealogists of morals, in the form in which they have existed until now, proceed in this matter? Naïvely, as they have always proceeded:—they find some 'aim' in punishment—revenge or deterrence, for example—then unsuspectingly posit this aim as the origin, as the *causa fiendi** of punishment, and then... leave it at that. But the 'lawful aim' is the last thing that should be used to investigate the history of the genesis of the law: there is, rather, no more important principle for all types of history than the following one, which it has taken such effort to acquire and furthermore really *should* be acquired by now—and that is, that there is a world of difference between the reason for something coming into existence in the first place and the ultimate use to which it is put, its actual application and integration into a system of goals; that anything which exists, once it has somehow come into being, can be reinterpreted in the service of new intentions, repossessed, repeatedly modified to a new use by a power superior to it; that everything which happens in the organic world is part of a process of *overpowering*, *mastering*, and that, in turn, all overpowering and mastering is a reinterpretation, a manipulation, in the course of which the previous 'meaning' and 'aim' must necessarily be obscured or completely effaced. No matter how well one has understood the *usefulness* of any physiological organ (or, for that matter, legal institution, social custom, political practice, artistic or religious form), one has learnt nothing about its origin in the process. I maintain this view regardless of the discomfort and displeasure it might cause to older ears—since from time immemorial it had been believed that in understanding the ascertainable aims and use of a thing, a form, an institution, one also understood why it had come into existence—thus the eye was understood as made for seeing, the hand as made for grasping. Similarly, punishment had been regarded as having been invented specifically for the purpose of punishing. But all aims, all uses are merely *signs* indicating that a will to power* has mastered something less powerful than itself and impressed the meaning of a function upon it in accordance with its own interests. So the entire history of a 'thing', an organ, a custom may take the form of an extended chain of signs, of ever-new interpretations and manipulations, whose causes do not themselves necessarily stand in relation to one another, but merely follow and replace one another arbitrarily and according to circumstance. The 'development' of a thing, a custom, an organ does not in the least resemble a *progressus** towards a goal, and even less the logical and shortest *progressus*, the most economical in terms of expenditure of force and cost. Rather, this development assumes the form of the succession of the more or less far-reaching, more or less independent processes of overpowering which affect it—including also in each case the resistance marshalled against these processes, the changes of form attempted with a view to defence and reaction, and the results of these successful counteractions. The form is fluid, but the 'meaning' even more so... Even within each individual organism the situation is no different: with each essential stage of growth of the whole, the 'meaning' of the individual organs also changes.* Under certain circumstances, the partial destruction or reduction in number of these individual organs (as, for example, through the elimination of connecting members) can be a sign of increasing strength and completion. By this I mean that partial *loss of use*, withering, degeneration, loss of meaning and expediency—in short, death—belongs to the conditions of true *progressus*, and as such always appears in the form of a will and a way to *greater power* and is always implemented at the expense of countless lesser powers. The extent of an 'advance' is even *measured* according to the scale of the sacrifice required; the mass of humanity sacrificed to the flourishing of a single *stronger* species of man—now that *would* be progress... I emphasize this central perspective of historical method all the more since it is fundamentally opposed to the prevailing instincts and tastes of the time, which would rather accommodate the absolute arbitrariness, even mechanistic senselessness of all that happens, than the theory of a *will to power* manifesting itself in all things and events. The idiosyncratic democratic prejudice against everything which dominates and wishes to dominate, this modern *misarchism** (to give an ugly name to an ugly development), has gradually disguised itself in the form of intelligence, the greatest intelligence, to the extent that it is now in the process of gradually infiltrating—has now been *allowed* to infiltrate—the most rigorous, and apparently most objective sciences. As far as I can see, it has already succeeded in dominating physiology and the study of life as a whole—to its detriment, as goes without saying—by conjuring away one of its basic concepts, that of essential *activity*. Instead, under pressure from the aforementioned idiosyncratic prejudice, the concept of 'adaptation'—a second-order activity, a mere reactivity—has been pushed to the forefront, and even life itself has been defined as an ever-more expedient inner adaptation to external circumstances (Herbert Spencer*). But this represents a failure to recognize the essence of life, its *will to power*; this overlooks the priority of the spontaneous, attacking, overcoming, reinterpreting, restructuring and shaping forces, whose action precedes 'adaptation'; this denies even the dominating role of the organism's highest functionaries, in which the vital will manifests itself actively and in its form-giving capacity. Remember what Huxley* reproached Spencer with—'administrative nihilism': but what is at issue here is *more* than just 'administration'...

13

—To return to the subject, to the issue of *punishment*, that is, there are two aspects of the problem to be distinguished: on the one hand, that aspect of punishment which is relatively *enduring*—the custom, the act, the 'drama', a certain strict sequence of procedures—and, on the other hand, that aspect which is *fluid*—the meaning, the aim, the expectation which is attached to the execution of such procedures. It is here simply presupposed, *per analogiam*,* in accordance with the central perspective of historical method which I have just elaborated, that the procedure itself will be something older, earlier than its use as a means of punishment, and that this use has only been *introduced* or interpreted into the procedure, which, having been in existence for some time, previously had another meaning and use. In short, it is presupposed that things are not as our naïve genealogists of morals and law have previously assumed, thinking as they all do that the procedure was *invented* specifically for the purpose of punishment—just as it was formerly thought that the hand was invented in order to grasp. As for that other element of punishment—the fluid aspect, its 'meaning'—in a very late stage of cultural development (as, for example, in contemporary Europe) the concept 'punishment' in fact no longer possesses a *single* meaning, but a whole synthesis of 'meanings'. The whole history of punishment up to this point, the history of its exploitation to the most diverse ends, finally crystallizes in a sort of unity which is difficult to unravel, difficult to analyse, and—a point which must be emphasized—completely *beyond definition*. (Nowadays it is impossible to say *why* people are punished: all concepts in which a whole process is summarized in signs escape definition; only that which is without history can be defined.*) In an earlier stage, however, this synthesis of 'meanings' seems less tightly bound together and more easily altered; one can still perceive how in each individual case the elements of the synthesis change their value and reorganize themselves accordingly, so that now one, now another element comes to the fore and dominates at the expense of the rest; even how under the right circumstances one element (say, the aim of deterrence) seems to cancel out all the others. In order to give at least an idea of how unsure, how retroactive, how accidental the 'meaning' of punishment is, and how one and the same procedure can be used, interpreted, and manipulated according to diametrically opposed intentions, here is the schema which I myself have come up with on the basis of a relatively small and arbitrary sample of material: punishment as a way of rendering harmless, of preventing further damage; punishment as compensation in any form to the victim for the harm done (also in the form of emotional compensation); punishment as the isolation of something which disturbs equilibrium, in order to prevent the disturbance from spreading; punishment as a means of instilling fear of those who determine and exact punishment; punishment as a form of forfeit due in return for the advantages which the criminal previously enjoyed (as, for example, when he is made useful as slave-labour in the mines); punishment as elimination of a degenerate element (in certain circumstances, of a whole branch, as in Chinese law: hence, as a means towards maintaining racial purity or a social type); punishment as festivity, that is, as the violation and humiliation of an enemy finally overcome; punishment as a means of producing a memory, whether for the person on whom the punishment is inflicted—so-called 'rehabilitation'—or for those who witness its execution; punishment as the payment of a remuneration stipulated by the power which then protects the wrongdoer from the excesses of revenge; punishment as a form of compromise with the natural condition of revenge, in so far as this state is still maintained by powerful races and claimed as a privilege; punishment as a declaration of war and implementation of a military strategy against an enemy of peace, law, order, authority, who, deemed dangerous to the community and in breach of contract with regard to its conditions, is combated as a rebel, traitor, and breaker of the peace with the very means offered by war itself.

14

This list is far from exhaustive; punishment is clearly overlaid with all sorts of uses. All the more reason to rule out an *alleged* use, albeit one which is popularly regarded as the most essential—and indeed this is where the faltering belief in punishment nowadays, for a variety of reasons, still finds its strongest support. Punishment is supposed to have the value of awakening the *sense of guilt* in the culprit, it is expected to be the actual *instrumentum** of the psychic reaction which is called 'bad conscience', 'pangs of conscience'. But this is to distort the reality and psychology of the present: and how much more this is the case when it comes to the longest period of human history, its prehistory! Genuine pangs of conscience are especially rare among criminals and prisoners, prisons and jails are far from being the preferred breeding-grounds of this species of gnawing worm—there is agreement on this point among all conscientious observers, who in many cases deliver such a judgement reluctantly enough and against their own wishes. Broadly speaking, punishment hardens and deadens: it concentrates; it intensifies the feeling of alienation; it strengthens resistance. If punishment does happen to sap a man's energy and bring about a wretched prostration and self-abasement, then such a result is certainly even more unpleasant than the average effect of punishment, which is dry and sombre seriousness. But if we bear in mind the *pre*-historical phase of mankind, then we may be quite safe in judging that it is the practice of punishment itself which has most powerfully *hindered* the development of this sense of guilt—at least with respect to the victims on whom the power of punishment is exercised. For let us not underestimate the extent to which the spectacle of the judicial and executive procedures themselves prevent the criminal from feeling his deed, his type of action to be reprehensible *as such*: for he sees exactly the same type of actions performed in the service of justice and as such approved, practised with good conscience: spying, deception, corruption, entrapment, the whole sly and cunning art of the police and the prosecutor. Not to mention the fundamental theft, assault, insult, imprisonment, torture, murder—practised in this instance as a matter of principle and without mitigating emotional circumstances—which appear in a pronounced manner in the various forms of punishment—all actions now in no way condemned and dismissed *as such* by his judges, but only from a certain perspective and in terms of a certain application. 'Bad conscience', this most sinister and most interesting plant of our earthly vegetation, did *not* grow up on this soil—in fact, throughout the longest period of history, those who judge and punish had no consciousness of dealing with a 'guilty' man, but rather with someone who causes harm, with an irresponsible piece of fate. And the man himself, on whom punishment subsequently descended, likewise like a piece of fate, experienced in the process no other 'inner suffering' than he might in the event of something unexpected suddenly occurring, of a terrifying natural phenomenon, of an avalanche, against which there is no possibility of defence.

15

This idea insinuated itself into Spinoza's mind once (to the annoyance of his interpreters, who go to great pains to misunderstand him on this point—take Kuno Fischer,* for example), when one afternoon, chafing on who knows what remembered incident, he pursued the question of what, for him, was left of the famous *morsus conscientiae**—he who had banished good and evil to the realm of human illusions and furiously defended the honour of his 'free' God against those blasphemers who asserted that God did everything *sub ratione boni** ('but that would be tantamount to subordinating God to fate and would in truth be the greatest of all absurdities'). The world for Spinoza had returned once again to that state of innocence in which it had lain before the invention of bad conscience: what had become of the *morsus conscientiae* in the process? 'The opposite of *gaudium*',* he said eventually—'a sadness accompanied by the memory of something in the past which took a completely unexpected turn.' *Eth. III propos. XVIII schol. I. II.* For thousands of years, evil-doers, once their punishment has caught up with them, have felt *no differently from Spinoza* as regards their 'misdemeanours': 'Something has gone unexpectedly wrong here', *not* 'I should not have done that'—they submitted to punishment, as one submits to an illness or to a misfortune or to death, with that brave and resigned fatalism which continues to represent the superiority of the Russian over the Western attitude to life. If in those days the deed was criticized, it was on grounds of prudence: we must without question look for the actual effect of punishment above all in a greater prudence, in a longer memory, in a determination to approach things more carefully, more suspiciously, more furtively in future, as well as in the realization that many things are definitively beyond one's strength, in a kind of improved self-evaluation. The broad effects of punishment in man and animal are increased fear, greater prudence, the mastering of desires: in this way punishment *tames* man, but it does not make him 'better'—one might with more justification assert the opposite. ('Pain makes one prudent', the common people say: in so far as it makes one prudent, it also makes one bad. Fortunately, it often enough makes one stupid into the bargain.)

16

At this point, I can no longer avoid giving my own hypothesis as to the origin of 'bad conscience' its first, provisional expression: it does not make for easy listening and requires a long period of continuous reflection and consideration, filling waking and sleeping hours. I take bad conscience to be the deep sickness to which man was obliged to succumb under the pressure of that most fundamental of all changes—when he found himself definitively locked in the spell of society and peace. These half-animals who were happily adapted to a life of wilderness, war, nomadism, and adventure were affected in a similar way to the creatures of the sea when they were forced either to adapt to life on land or to perish—in a single stroke, all their instincts were devalued and 'suspended'. From that moment on they had to walk on their feet and 'support themselves', where previously they had been supported by water: a horrific weight bore down on them. The simplest tasks made them feel clumsy, they were without their old guides in this new, unknown world, the regulating drives with their instinctive certainty—they were reduced, these unfortunate creatures, to thinking, drawing conclusions, calculating, combining causes and effects, to their 'consciousness', their most meagre and unreliable organ! I believe that never on earth had there been such a feeling of misery, such leaden discomfort. Nor did the old instincts all of a sudden cease making their demands! Only it was difficult and seldom possible to obey them: for the most part, they had to seek new and, at the same time, subterranean satisfactions for themselves. Every instinct which does not vent itself externally *turns inwards*—this is what I call the *internalization* of man: it is at this point that what is later called the 'soul' first develops in man. The whole inner world, originally stretched thinly as between two membranes, has been extended and expanded, has acquired depth, breadth, and height in proportion as the external venting of human instinct has been *inhibited*. Those fearful bulwarks by means of which the state organization protected itself against the old instincts of freedom—punishment belongs above all to these bulwarks—, caused all the instincts of the wild, free, nomadic man to turn backwards *against man himself*. Hostility, cruelty, pleasure in persecution, in assault, in change, in destruction,—all that turning against the man who possesses such instincts: *such* is the origin of 'bad conscience'. The man who is forced into an oppressively narrow and regular morality, who for want of external enemies and resistance impatiently tears, persecutes, gnaws, disturbs, mistreats himself, this animal which is to be 'tamed', which rubs himself raw on the bars of his cage, this deprived man consumed with homesickness for the desert, who had no choice but to transform himself into an adventure, a place of torture, an uncertain and dangerous wilderness—this fool, this yearning and desperate prisoner became the inventor of 'bad conscience'. But with him was introduced the greatest and most sinister sickness which still afflicts man even today, man's suffering *from man*, *from himself*: this as a result of a violent separation from his animal past, of a leap which is also a fall into new situations and conditions of existence, of a declaration of war against the old instincts, which previously constituted the basis of his strength, pleasure, and fearfulness. On the other hand, let us add immediately that with the emergence of an animal soul turned against itself and taking sides against itself, something so new, so deep, so unprecedented, so enigmatic *and pregnant with the future* came into existence that the earth's aspect was essentially altered. In fact, it took divine spectators to appreciate fully the drama which began at that time and whose end is not yet in sight, not by a long way—a drama too fine, too marvellous, too paradoxical to be allowed to run senselessly unnoticed on just any ridiculous star! Since that time, man *counts* among the most unexpected and exciting lucky throws of the dice played by Heraclitus' 'great child'*—whether that be Zeus or chance—he arouses interest, suspense, hope, almost certainty, as if in him something were being announced, were being prepared, as if man were not an end in himself, but rather only a pathway, an incident, a bridge, a great promise...

17

This hypothesis as to the origin of bad conscience presupposes first that this change was not gradual and voluntary, an organic growth into new conditions, but rather a break, a leap, a compulsion, an irrefutable fate, against which there was no struggle nor even any *ressentiment*. And secondly, that the insertion of a previously unrestrained and unshaped population into a fixed form, just as it began with an act of violence, was only brought to completion through simple acts of violence—that the oldest 'state' accordingly emerged and endured as a fearful tyranny, as a crushing and thoughtless machinery, until such a raw material of common people and half-animals was finally not only thoroughly kneaded and malleable but also *formed*. I used the word 'state': it goes without saying what I mean by that—some horde or other of blond predatory animals, a race of conquerors and masters which, itself organized for war and with the strength to organize others, unhesitatingly lays its fearful paws on a population which may be hugely superior in numerical terms but remains shapeless and nomadic. Such is the beginning of the 'state' on earth: I think that the sentimental effusion which suggested that it originates in a 'contract'* has been done away with. He who is capable of giving commands, who is a 'master' by nature, who behaves violently in deed and gesture—what are contracts to him! One does not reckon with such beings, they arrive like fate, without motive, reason, consideration, pretext, they arrive like lightning, too fearful, too sudden, too convincing, too 'different', even to be hated. Their work is an instinctive creation and impression of form, they are the most involuntary, most unconscious artists there are—wherever they appear, something new quickly grows up, a *living* structure of domination, in which parts and functions are demarcated and articulated, where only that which has first been given a 'meaning' with respect to the whole finds a place. The meaning of guilt, responsibility, and consideration is unknown to these born organizers; the fearful egoism of the artist presides in them, with its gaze of bronze and sense of being justified in advance to all eternity in its 'work', like the mother in her child. *They* were not the ones among whom 'bad conscience' grew up, as goes without saying from the outset—but it would not have grown up *without them*, this ugly weed, it would not exist if, under the force of their hammer-blows, of their artists' violence, a vast quantity of freedom had not been expelled from the world, or at least removed from visibility and, as it were, forcibly made *latent*. This *instinct of freedom* made latent through force—as we have already understood—this instinct of freedom, forced back, trodden down, incarcerated within and ultimately still venting and discharging itself only upon itself: such is *bad conscience* at its origin, that and nothing more.

18

So one should take care not to think any the worse of this entire phenomenon because it is from the outset ugly and painful. It is basically the same active force as is more impressively at work in the artists of force and organizers who build states. But here, on the inside, on a smaller, meaner scale, in the reverse direction, in the 'labyrinth of the breast', to use Goethe's words,* it creates for itself a bad conscience and builds negative ideals. It is that very same *instinct of freedom* (in my terminology: the will to power): except that the material on which the form-creating and violating nature of this force vents itself is in this case man himself, the whole of his old animal self—and *not*, as is the case with that greater and more conspicuous phenomenon, the *other* man, *other* men. This secret self-violation, this artistic cruelty, this desire to give a form to the refractory, resistant, suffering material of oneself, to brand oneself with a will, a criticism, a contradiction, a contempt, a No, this sinister labour, both horrific and pleasurable, of a soul voluntarily divided against itself, a soul which makes itself suffer for the pleasure of it, this whole *active* 'bad conscience', this actual maternal womb of ideal and imaginative events, has ultimately—as will be clear by now—brought to light much that is new and disturbing in the way of beauty and affirmation, and perhaps even first brought to light beauty *as such*... For what would the meaning of 'beautiful' be, if contradiction had not first become conscious of itself, if the ugly had not first said to itself: 'I am ugly'?... After this hint, at least, the enigma of how contradictory concepts like *selflessness*, *self-denial*, *self-sacrifice* can suggest an ideal, a beauty, will be less enigmatic. One thing is certain from now on, I have no doubt—that is, the kind of pleasure the selfless, the self-denying, the self-sacrificing man feels from the outset: this pleasure belongs to cruelty.—So much provisionally on the subject of the origin of the 'unegoistic' as a *moral* value and of the concealment of the ground on which this value has grown: only bad conscience, only the will to mistreat the self supplies the condition for the *value* of the unegoistic.—

19

Bad conscience is an illness, there is no doubt about it, but an illness in the same way that pregnancy is an illness. Let us seek the conditions under which this illness has attained its most fearful and most sublime peak—then we will see what actually made its entry into the world at this point. But for that a deep breath is required—and as a first step we must return to an earlier point of view. The private legal relationship between debtor and creditor which we have discussed earlier has been interpreted, in a manner which, when viewed from a historical perspective, strikes one as extremely alien and disturbing, into a relationship where we modern men perhaps have the greatest difficulty in grasping its relevance: that is, into the relationship of the *present generation* to its *forefathers*. Within the original race-community—we are talking about the very earliest times—the living generation always recognizes a juridical obligation towards the earlier generation, and particularly towards the earliest generation, which founded the race (and this is in no way merely an emotional tie: there may even be grounds to dispute the existence of such a tie as regards the longest period of the history of mankind). Here the conviction prevails that the race only *exists* by virtue of the sacrifice and achievements of the forefathers—and that one is obliged to *repay* them through sacrifice and achievements: a *debt* is recognized, which gnaws incessantly by virtue of the fact that these forefathers, in their continued existence as powerful spirits, never cease to grant the race new advantages and advances in strength. Are these given gratis, then? But there is no such thing as 'gratis' for this raw period which 'lacks soul'. What can be given them in return? Sacrifices (initially as food, in terms of the crudest understanding), festivities, choirs, salutes, above all obedience—for all customs are, as the work of the forefathers, also their rules and commands—: does one ever give them enough? This suspicion persists and grows: from time to time it exacts a large lump repayment, something horrific by way of remuneration to the 'creditor' (the notorious sacrifice of the first-born, for example—blood, human blood, in any case). According to this kind of logic, the *fear* of the forefather and of his power, the consciousness of indebtedness towards him necessarily increases in exact proportion as the power of the race itself increases, as the race itself becomes ever-more victorious, independent, respected, feared. And not somehow the other way round! Every step towards the withering of the race, all the arbitrary miseries, all signs of degeneration, of approaching dissolution always rather *reduce* the fear of the spirit of the founder and give rise to an ever-weaker impression of his wisdom, foresight, and powerful presence. If one thinks this crude kind of logic through to its conclusion, then finally the forefathers of the *most powerful* races would have to grow to a monstrous scale in the eyes of an increasingly fearful imagination and retreat into the darkness of what is divinely sinister and inconceivable—ultimately, the forefather is necessarily transfigured into a *god*. Perhaps this is where the gods originate, then—from *fear*!... And whoever should deem it necessary to add: 'but from piety as well!' would be hard-pressed to justify this as regards the longest period of the history of the human race, the very earliest times. And even more so admittedly as regards the *middle* period, in which the noble races develop themselves—and who as such, in fact, repay their founding fathers, their ancestors (heroes, gods) with interest, in terms of all the qualities which in the meantime have been revealed in themselves, the *noble* qualities. Later we will take another look at the ennobling and refining of the gods (which is certainly not to be equated with their becoming 'holy'). But for the moment let us bring our account of the course of this entire development of the sense of guilt to a provisional conclusion.

20

As history teaches us, the sense of being indebted to the deity by no means came to an end with the decline of the organization of 'community' according to kinship. Just as it has inherited the concepts 'good and bad' from the nobility of the race (along with its basic psychological propensity to establish hierarchies), mankind has inherited along with the gods of the race and the tribe the burden of its still-outstanding debts and the desire to have them redeemed. (The transition is effected by those widespread slave and serf populations which have adapted themselves to the divine cult of their masters, whether through compulsion or through submissiveness and *mimicry*:* from them this legacy then overflows in all directions.) The sense of guilt towards the divinity has continued to grow for several thousands of years, and always in the same proportion as the concept and sense of god has grown and risen into the heights. (The whole history of ethnic strife, victory, reconciliation, fusion, everything which precedes the definitive rank-ordering of all the elements of a people in that great synthesis of races, is mirrored in the tangled genealogies of its gods, in the myths of their struggles, victories, and reconciliations; the progress of universal empires is always the progress towards universal divinities, the triumph of despotism over the independent nobility always prepares the way for some monotheism or other.) The arrival of the Christian God, as the uttermost example of godliness so far realized on earth, has brought with it the phenomenon of the uttermost sense of guilt. Assuming that we have subsequently begun to move in the *opposite* direction, we might very probably deduce from the inexorable decline of faith in the Christian God that by now the human sense of guilt should have weakened considerably. Indeed, the prospect that the complete and definitive victory of atheism might redeem mankind entirely from this feeling of indebtedness towards its origins, its *causa prima*,* cannot be dismissed. Atheism and a kind of *second innocence* belong together.—

21

So much briefly by way of a provisional note on the relationship between religious presuppositions and the concepts of 'guilt' and 'duty'. So far, I have deliberately left aside the actual moralization of these concepts (the way these same concepts are pushed back into the conscience; to be more precise, the entanglement of *bad* conscience with the concept of God) and at the end of the previous paragraph even talked as if this moralization had not taken place, and consequently, as if these concepts were from now on necessarily approaching their end, now that their pre-condition, the belief in our 'creditor', in God, has collapsed. The real situation is fearfully different. The moralization of the concepts guilt and duty, their being pushed back into *bad* conscience, actually represents an attempt to *reverse* the direction of the development just described, or at least to halt its movement. The *goal* now is the pessimistic one of closing off once and for all the prospect of a definitive repayment, the *goal* now is to make the gaze ricochet, recoil inconsolably from an iron impossibility, the *goal* now is to turn those concepts 'guilt' and 'duty' back—against *whom* then? There can be no doubt: first against the 'debtor', in whom from now on bad conscience takes root, eating its way in, spreading down and out like a polyp, until finally, along with the irredeemability of guilt, the irredeemability of penance, the thought of the impossibility of repayment (of '*eternal* punishment') is conceived. But ultimately these concepts are turned back even against the 'creditor', whether one has in mind the *causa prima* of man, the beginning of the human race, its forefather, who is from now on tainted by a curse ('Adam', 'original sin', 'lack of free will'), or nature, from whose womb man developed and into which from now on the principle of evil is introduced ('demonization of nature'), or existence itself, which survives as *essentially devoid of value* (the nihilistic renunciation of existence, the desire for nothingness or desire for its 'opposite', a different way of being, Buddhism and related matters)—until all at once we find ourselves standing in front of the horrific and paradoxical expedient in which tortured humanity has found a temporary relief, that stroke of genius on the part of *Christianity*: God sacrificing himself for the guilt of man, God paying himself off, God as the sole figure who can redeem on man's behalf that which has become irredeemable for man himself—the creditor sacrificing himself for his debtor, out of *love* (are we supposed to believe this?—), out of love for his debtor!...

22

Exactly *what* has happened here *underneath* all this will already be clear: the will to self-torture, that downtrodden cruelty of the internalized animal man who has been chased back into himself, of the man locked up in the 'state' in order to be tamed, the man who invented bad conscience in order to inflict pain on himself after the *more natural* outlet for this desire to inflict pain was obstructed—this man of bad conscience has assumed control of the religious presupposition in order to carry his self-punishment to the most horrific pitch of harsh intensity. Indebtedness towards *God*: this thought becomes for him an instrument of torture. In 'God' he apprehends the ultimate opposing principle to his actual and irredeemable animal instincts, he himself reinterprets these animal instincts as a debt towards God (as hostility, rebellion, revolt against the 'master', the 'father', the original founding father and beginning of the world), he stretches himself on the rack of the contradiction between 'God' and 'Devil', he expels from himself every negation of himself, of nature, the natural, the reality of his being, in the form of an affirmation, as something which exists, as incarnate, real, as God, as God's holiness, as God's judgement, as God's punishment, as the beyond, as eternity, as suffering without end, as hell, as immeasurability of punishment and guilt. This represents a kind of madness of the will in psychic cruelty which simply knows no equal: the *will* of man to find himself guilty and reprehensible to a point beyond the possibility of atonement, his *will* to think himself punished without the punishment ever being commensurate with his guilt, his *will* to infect and poison things to their very depths with the problem of punishment and guilt, in order to cut off once and for all any escape from this labyrinth of *idées fixes*, his *will* to establish an ideal—that of the 'holy God'—, and to feel the palpable certainty of his absolute unworthiness with respect to that ideal. Oh this insane, sad beast, man! What things occur to him, what unnatural things, what absurd paroxysms, what *bestiality of the idea* breaks out immediately if he is even as much as slightly hindered from being a *beast of the deed*!... This is all extremely interesting, but also of such black, sombre, unnerving sadness that one must forcibly restrain oneself from gazing into these abysses for too long. There is *sickness* here, without doubt, the most fearful sickness which up until now has raged in man—and anyone who can still hear (although nowadays no one has the ears to hear it any more!—) how in this night of torment and absurdity the cry of *love*, the scream of the most yearning delight, of redemption in *love* has resounded, he turns away, seized by an uncontrollable horror... In man there is so much that is horrific!... The earth has been a madhouse for too long already!...

23

Let that suffice once and for all on the subject of the origin of the 'holy God'.—That the *conception* of gods need not in itself necessarily lead to the deterioration of the imagination, which we have been obliged to consider briefly, that there are *nobler* ways of making use of the invention of gods than to the end of the self-crucifixion and self-defilement of man in which the latter centuries of European history have displayed their mastery—this, fortunately, is revealed by the merest glance at the *Greek gods*, those reflections of noble and self-controlled man, in whom the *animal* in man felt himself deified and did *not* tear himself apart, did *not* rage against himself! Throughout the longest period of their history the Greeks used their gods for no other purpose than to keep 'bad conscience' at bay, to be allowed to enjoy the freedom of their soul: thus, in a sense diametrically opposed to that in which Christianity has made use of its God. They went *very far* in this direction, these magnificent child-minds with the courage of lions; and no lesser authority than that of the Homeric Zeus himself on occasion gives them to understand that they are making things too easy for themselves. 'It is a wonder!' he says on one occasion—at issue is the case of Aegisthos,* a *very* serious case—'It is a wonder how much mortals complain about the gods! They allege that evil comes only from us; but they are the authors of their own misery, even contrary to fate, through lack of reason.' Yet it is immediately clear how far even this Olympian spectator and judge is from bearing a grudge and being ill-disposed to them as a result: 'How *silly* they are!' is what he thinks of the misdeeds of mortals—and 'foolishness', 'lack of judgement', a little 'rush of blood to the head'—the Greeks of the strongest, boldest period have themselves *admitted* as much as the reason for a great deal of what is bad and disastrous—foolishness, *not* sin! do you follow?... But even this rush of blood to the head posed a problem—'Yes, how is it possible? what might actually cause it in the case of heads such as *ours*, as men of noble origin, of good fortune, we men of good constitution, of the best society, of nobility, of virtue?' For centuries, the refined Greek asked himself such questions when confronted with an incomprehensible atrocity and wanton crime with which one of his own had tainted himself. 'A *god* must have beguiled him', he said to himself finally, shaking his head... This expedient is *typical* of the Greeks... Thus the gods at that time served to justify man even to a certain extent in wicked actions, they served as the cause of evil—at that time they did not take upon themselves the execution of punishment, but rather, as is *nobler*, the guilt...

24

—I conclude with three question-marks, that much seems clear. 'Is an ideal actually being set up or broken down here?' I may be asked... But have you ever asked yourselves often enough how much the setting up of *every* single ideal on earth has cost? How much reality had to be defamed and denied, how many lies sanctified, how much conscience disturbed, how much 'god' sacrificed each time to that end? In order for a shrine to be set up, *another shrine must be broken into pieces*: that is the law—show me the case where it is not so!... We modern men, we are the heirs to centuries of the vivisection of conscience and animal self-torture: it is in this that we have our greatest experience, our artistry perhaps, in any case, our refinement, the luxury which vitiates our taste. For all too long man has looked askance at his natural inclinations, with the result that they have ultimately become interwoven with 'bad conscience'. An attempt at reversal would *in itself* be possible—but who is strong enough to undertake it?—that is, an attempt instead to interweave bad conscience with the *unnatural* inclinations, all those aspirations to the beyond, the absurd, the anti-instinctual, the anti-animal, in short, to what have up to now been regarded as ideals, ideals which are all hostile to life, ideals which defame the world. To whom can one turn today with *such* hopes and demands?... The good men are the very people who would oppose it; as would, of course, the comfortable, the reconciled, the vain, the sentimentally effusive, the exhausted men... What is more deeply insulting to them, what isolates us more completely from them than to reveal a glimpse of our self-discipline and self-respect? And again—how accommodating, how kind the whole world shows itself to us, as soon as we behave like everyone else and 'let ourselves go' like everyone else!... Such a goal would require *different* kinds of spirit than are likely in this period, of all periods: spirits, who, strengthened through wars and victories, have developed a need for conquest, adventure, danger, pain; it would require acclimatization to sharp, high-altitude air, to winter expeditions, to ice and mountains in every sense, it would even require a kind of sublime wickedness, a last, self-assured intellectual malice which belongs to great health, it would require, in short—and which is bad enough—nothing less than this *great health* itself!... Is this still possible even today?... But at some time, in a period stronger than this brittle, self-doubting present, he must yet come to us, the *redeemer* of great love and contempt, the creative spirit whose compelling strength allows him no rest in any remote retreat and beyond, a spirit whose seclusion is misunderstood by the common people, as if it were a flight *from* reality—while it is only a further steeping, burrowing, plunging *into* reality, from which he may at some time return to the light, bearing the *redemption* of this reality: its redemption from the curse which the previous ideal has laid upon it. This man of the future, who will redeem us as much from the previous ideal as from *what was bound to grow out of it*, from the great disgust, from the will to nothingness, from nihilism, this midday stroke of the bell, this toll of great decision, which once again liberates the will, which once again gives the earth its goal and man his hope, this Antichristian* and Antinihilist, this conqueror of God and of nothingness—*he must come one day*...

25

—But what am I saying here? Enough! Enough! At this point only one thing is fitting, to keep silent: otherwise I would interfere with what only a younger man is at liberty to do, someone 'more pregnant with the future', someone stronger than I am—something which only *Zarathustra** is at liberty to do, *Zarathustra the godless*...

THIRD ESSAY

What is the Meaning of Ascetic Ideals?

> Unconcerned, contemptuous, violent—this is how wisdom would have *us* be: she is a woman, she only ever loves a warrior.
>
> *Thus Spake Zarathustra**

1

What is the meaning of ascetic ideals?—In the case of artists, nothing or too many things; in the case of philosophers and intellectuals, something like an instinctive sense for the preconditions favourable to higher spirituality; in the case of women, yet *another* seductive charm, a little *morbidezza** in beautiful flesh, the angelic character of a plump and pretty animal; in the case of the deformed and the disgruntled (the *majority* of mortals), an attempt to imagine oneself 'too good' for this world, a holy form of dissipation, their principal means in the struggle against chronic pain and boredom; in the case of priests, the distinctive priestly belief, its most effective instrument of power, also the 'very highest' licence for power; in the case of saints finally, a pretext for hibernation, their *novissima gloriae cupido*,* their rest in nothingness ('God'), their form of madness. But *that* the ascetic ideal has meant so many things to man expresses above all the fundamental truth about human will, its *horror vacui:* it must have a goal*—and it would even will *nothingness* rather than *not* will at all.—Do you follow?... Have you been following?... '*Certainly not! Sir!*'—Then let us start from the beginning.

2

What is the meaning of ascetic ideals?—Or, to take an individual case on which I am frequently consulted, what does it mean, for example, when an artist like Richard Wagner* pays homage to chastity in his old age? In a certain sense, admittedly, he has never done anything else; but only right at the end did he do so in an ascetic sense. What does it mean, this change of 'meaning', this radical reversal of meaning?—for it was nothing less than that, and through it Wagner at a single stroke transformed himself directly into his opposite. What does it mean when an artist transforms himself into his opposite in this way?... If we are willing to pause for a moment at this question, what was perhaps the best, strongest, happiest, *most courageous* time in Wagner's life will immediately come to mind: the time when he was profoundly occupied with the thought of Luther's wedding.* Who knows to what chance events we owe the fact that today we possess the *Meistersinger** rather than this wedding music? And who knows how much of the latter still rings through the former? But there is no doubt that this *Luther's Wedding* would have been another hymn to chastity. Admittedly, a hymn to sensuality too—and in that respect it would seem to me quite proper, in that respect it would have been 'Wagnerian'. For there is no necessary opposition between chastity and sensuality; every good marriage, every real love from the heart is beyond this opposition. Wagner would have done well, it seems to me, to remind his Germans of this *pleasant* fact with the aid of a sweet and bold Luther comedy, for there have always been—and there still are—many Germans who defame sensuality. Perhaps Luther's merit lies in nothing greater than in his having had the courage of his *sensuality* (—in those days it went by the delicate enough name of the 'Protestant freedom'...). But fortunately, even in cases where there is a real opposition between chastity and sensuality, it need no longer be a tragic one. This should hold at least for all well-constituted and well-disposed mortals, who are far from simply regarding their delicate equilibrium between 'animal and angel' as one of the arguments against existence—the finest and brightest, like Goethe, like Hafis,* have even seen it as a *further* stimulus to life. Such 'contradictions' belong to the very seductions of existence... On the other hand, it is only too evident that once the unsuccessful swine are brought to the point of worshipping chastity—and such swine do exist!—they will see and worship in it only their antithesis, the antithesis of the unsuccessful swine—and with what tragic, grunting enthusiasm! One can imagine the embarrassing and superfluous antithesis which at the end of his life it was Richard Wagner's indisputable intention to set to music and put on stage. *But to what purpose?* one may reasonably ask. For what are the swine to him, what are they to us?—

3

Here admittedly one cannot avoid that other question, the question as to what that manly (oh, so unmanly) 'village idiot', that poor devil and country lad Parsifal* was to him, Parsifal, whom he finally with such insidious means made Catholic—what? was this Parsifal meant to be taken at all *seriously*? For one might be tempted to suspect, even to wish, the opposite—that Wagner's Parsifal was meant as a joke, as an epilogue and satyr play,* so to speak, with which the tragedian Wagner wanted to take his leave of us, of himself, above all, of *tragedy*, in a fitting and worthy way, that is to say, in an excess of the highest and most mischievous parody of the tragic itself, of the whole horror of earthly seriousness and misery as it has existed from time immemorial, of the *crudest form*, now overcome at last, assumed by the unnatural ascetic ideal. That, as I said, would have been worthy of a great tragedian; he, like all artists, only reaches the peak of his greatness once he is capable of looking *down* on himself and his art—once he is capable of *laughing* at himself. Is Wagner's *Parsifal* his secret superior laughter at himself, the triumph of his achievement of the ultimate, highest artistic freedom, artistic transcendence? One would, as I said, wish it so; for what would Parsifal be if *meant seriously*? Must one really see in him (as was once suggested to me) 'the monstrous product of an insane hatred of knowledge, spirit, and sensuality'? A curse on both the senses and the spirit in a *single* breath of hatred? A recantation and return to the sickly ideals of Christianity and obscurantism? And finally, even a denial of the self, a crossing-out of the self on the part of an artist who had previously been striving with his utmost will for the very opposite, that is, for the *highest spiritualization* *and sensualization** of his art? And not only of his art: but also of his life. Remember the enthusiasm with which Wagner in his time followed in the footsteps of the philosopher Feuerbach:* Feuerbach's motto of 'healthy sensuality'—in the 'thirties and 'forties that sounded to Wagner as it did to many Germans (—they called themselves the '*young* Germans'*) like the slogan of redemption. Has he finally *learnt otherwise*? Since it seems at least that he finally had the will to *teach otherwise*... And not only from the stage with the trombones of Parsifal—in the dark scribbling of his last years, as constrained as it is helpless, there are hundreds of places where a secret desire and will, a despondent, uncertain, inadmissable will reveals itself, a will to preach recantation, conversion, denial, Christianity, Middle Ages, and to say to his disciples: 'It is no use! look elsewhere for salvation!' He even invokes the 'blood of the redeemer' at one point...

4

If I might state my opinion on such a very embarrassing case—and it is a *typical* case—: one does well to separate the artist from his work, which should be taken more seriously than he is. Ultimately, he is no more than its pre-condition, the womb, the soil, possibly the manure and midden upon which, from which it grows—and thus, in most cases, something which must be forgotten before the work itself can be enjoyed. Insight into the origin of a work is a matter for physiologists and vivisectors of the spirit: but never one for the aesthetic men, the artists! The poet and creator of the *Parsifal* is not spared a deep, fundamental, even frightening growth and descent into medieval contrasts of the soul, a hostile remoteness from all elevation, strictness, and discipline of the spirit, a kind of intellectual *perversity* (if you will pardon the expression), just as a woman with child is not spared the repulsive and strange aspects of pregnancy: which, as I said, must be *forgotten* before the child can be enjoyed. One should be wary of confusion on the grounds of psychological *contiguity*,* to use the English terminology, a confusion into which an artist himself only too easily falls: as if he himself *were* what he is able to present, conceive, and express. *If*, in fact, this were the case, the artist simply would not present, conceive, and express the things he does; a Homer would have created no Achilles, a Goethe no Faust, if Homer had been an Achilles and Goethe a Faust. A complete and whole artist finds himself separated from the 'real', the actual, to all eternity. On the other hand, one can understand how he may tire, even despair, of the eternal 'unreality' and falsity of his innermost existence—and how he may then attempt to reach over into the very sphere which is most forbidden to him, into the real, how he may attempt to *exist* in reality. With what degree of success? It is not hard to guess... This is the *typical whim* of the artist: the same whim which befell the aged Wagner with such disastrous effects and cost him so dearly (—through it, he lost those of his friends who were of any worth). But ultimately, and quite apart from this whim, who would not wish, above all for Wagner's own sake, that he had taken leave of us and his art in a different way, not with a *Parsifal*, but in a more victorious, more self-assured, more Wagnerian way—in a way less misleading, less ambiguous with respect to what he wanted as a whole, a way less Schopenhauerian, less nihilistic?...

5

—What is the meaning of ascetic ideals, then? In the case of an artist, as we appreciate immediately: they mean *absolutely nothing!*... Or so many things as to amount to absolutely nothing!... Let us first eliminate the artists: for some time now, these artists have lacked sufficient independence in the world and in their stance *towards* the world for their value-judgements and re-evaluations to merit attention *in their own right*! They have always acted as valets to some ethics or philosophy or religion; not to mention the unfortunate fact that they have often been the all-too malleable courtiers of their supporters and patrons, sycophants with a fine nose for established powers or those just newly emerging. At the very least, they are always in need of protection, support, an authority which is already grounded: artists never take a stand on their own account, to stand alone goes against their deepest instincts. Thus Richard

Wagner, for example, stood behind the philosopher Schopenhauer, as his vanguard and protection, 'when the time came'—who could think it even conceivable that he would have had the *courage* to adopt an ascetic ideal without the support which Schopenhauer's philosophy offered him, without the authority of Schopenhauer which came to *dominate* Europe in the 'seventies? (and this without even considering the question of whether in the *new* Germany an artist would have been at all possible without the milk of human, imperially human kindness*).—And so we have arrived at the more serious question: what does it mean when the ascetic ideal is acclaimed by a genuine *philosopher*, a real self-reliant spirit like Schopenhauer's, a man and knight with an iron gaze, who has the courage to be himself, who is able to stand alone and does not wait first for a vanguard, for higher indications?—But at this point let us first consider an issue which fascinates many people, the peculiar stance which Schopenhauer adopted towards *art*: for this was patently the reason why Richard Wagner first went over to Schopenhauer (persuaded to do so by a poet, as one knows—Herwegh*), even to the extent of tearing open an unbridgeable theoretical rift between his earlier and his later aesthetic beliefs—the former as expressed, for example, in *Opera and Drama*, the latter in the writings which he published from 1870 on. In particular, and this is what is perhaps most alienating, from that moment on Wagner altered his judgement of the value and place of *music* itself without so much as a second thought: what did it matter to him that he had previously made music a means, a medium, a 'woman' who simply needed a goal, a man—that is, drama!—in order to thrive. He understood immediately that Schopenhauer's innovative theory meant that *more* could be done *in majorem musicae gloriam**—that is, with the *sovereignty* of music as Schopenhauer understood it: music placed on one side over against all the other arts, the independent art in itself, *not*, like the others, offering copies of the phenomenal world, but rather speaking the language *of* the will itself, directly from the 'abyss', as its most authentic, most original, least derived revelation. With this extraordinary inflation in the value of music, which seemed to follow from Schopenhauer's philosophy, *the musician* too suddenly rose in value: from that moment on he became an oracle, a priest, even more than a priest, a sort of spokesman of the 'in itself' of things,* a telephone of the beyond—from that time on he ceased to talk just music, this ventriloquist of God—he talked metaphysics: is it any wonder that one day he finally talked *ascetic ideals*?...

6

Schopenhauer made use of the Kantian version of the aesthetic problem*—although he certainly did not view it through Kantian eyes. Kant thought that he was doing art an honour by preferring and pushing to the forefront as predicates of the beautiful those characteristics which constituted the glory of knowledge: impersonality and universal validity. This is not the place to discuss whether this was not for the most part a mistake: the only thing I wish to emphasize is that Kant, instead of viewing the aesthetic problem from the experience of the artist (the creator), like all philosophers considered art and the beautiful exclusively from the point of view of the 'spectator', and in the process unwittingly included the 'spectator' himself in the concept 'beautiful'. But if only the philosophers of the beautiful had been sufficiently familiar with this 'spectator' at least!—that is, as a great *personal* fact and experience, as an abundance of the most authentic, intense experiences, desires, surprises, delights in the domain of the beautiful! But the opposite has, as I feared, always been the case: and so right from the outset they give us definitions within which, as in each of Kant's famous definitions of the beautiful, the lack of a more differentiated experience of the self sits like a fat worm of fundamental error. 'That which pleases *without interest*', Kant has said, 'is beautiful.' Without interest! Compare this definition with that offered by a genuine 'spectator' and artist—Stendhal, who once described the beautiful as *une promesse de bonheur*.* Here in any case the very aspect of the aesthetic condition which Kant emphasized at the expense of all others—*le désintéressement*—is rejected and crossed out. Who is right, Kant or Stendhal?—If our aestheticians admittedly never tire of arguing on Kant's behalf that under the spell of beauty it is possible to contemplate *even* statues of naked women 'without interest', one is entitled to have a little laugh at their expense—the experiences of the *artists* are on this thorny issue 'more interesting', and Pygmalion* was in any case *not* necessarily an 'unaesthetic man'. Let us think all the more highly of the innocence of our aestheticians as it is reflected in such arguments, let us, for example, count to Kant's credit the way in which he is able to discuss, with the naïveté of a country vicar, the particular qualities of the sense of touch!*—And here we return to Schopenhauer, whose close relationship to the arts was of a completely different order from Kant's and yet failed to escape the spell of the Kantian definition: how did that come about? The circumstance is surprising enough: he interpreted the phrase 'without interest' in the most personal way, on the basis of what must have been part of his most routine experience. Schopenhauer talks about few things with as much assurance as he does about the effect of aesthetic contemplation: he says of it that it actually counteracts *sexual* 'interest', like lupulin and camphor; he never tired of glorifying *this* liberation from the 'will' as the great advantage and use of the aesthetic condition. One might even be tempted to enquire whether his fundamental conception of 'will and representation', the thought that only 'representation' can offer redemption from the 'will', did not originate from a generalization of that sexual experience.* (By the way, in all questions relating to Schopenhauer's philosophy, it should never be forgotten that it is the conception of a young man of 26; so that it shares not only in what is specific to Schopenhauer but also in what is specific to that time of life.) Let us listen, for example, to one of the most emphatic of the countless passages which he wrote in praise of the aesthetic condition (*World as Will and Representation*, III, §38), let us isolate the tone, the suffering, the happiness, the gratitiude with which such words are spoken: 'This is the painless condition which Epicurus* praised as the highest good and the condition of the gods; for that moment, we are free from the base compulsion of the will, we celebrate the Sabbath after the hard labour of desire, the wheel of Ixion* stands still'... What vehemence of expression! What images of pain and enduring frustration! What a contrast, verging on the pathological, between the time of 'that moment' and what is otherwise the 'wheel of Ixion', the 'hard labour of desire', the 'base compulsion of the will'!—But assuming that Schopenhauer were a hundred times right as far as he himself was concerned, what meaning does this hold as an insight into the essence of the beautiful? Schopenhauer has described one effect of the beautiful, the calming of the will—but is this effect universal? As I said, Stendhal, a no-less sensual but more happily constituted nature than Schopenhauer, emphasizes a different effect of the beautiful: 'The beautiful is a *promise* of happiness.' For him, the fact of the matter seemed to be that the effect of the beautiful was none other than to *arouse the will* ('interest'). And might one not ultimately raise the objection that Schopenhauer was extremely mistaken to think himself a Kantian in this respect, that his understanding of Kant's definition of the beautiful was far from Kantian—that the pleasure of the beautiful was for him too one of 'interest', even one of the very strongest, most personal interest; that of the tortured man who is freed from his torture?... And, to return to our first question, 'what does it *mean* when a philosopher praises the ascetic ideal?'—we receive here at least a first hint: he wishes to be *freed from a form of torture*.

7

Let us not grow despondent at the mention of the word 'torture'; in this instance particularly, there is enough to set off against it, to mitigate it—even something to laugh about. In particular, let us not underestimate the fact that Schopenhauer, who actually treated sexuality (including its instrument, woman, that '*instrumentum diaboli*'*) as a personal enemy, *needed* enemies to remain in good spirits; that he loved grim, green, galling words; that he raged for the sake of raging, out of passion; that he would have fallen ill, become a *pessimist* (—for that he was not, however much he may have wanted to be one) without his enemies, without Hegel,* woman, sensuality, and the whole will to existence, the will to endure. Otherwise, Schopenhauer would *not* have endured, one may bet on that, he would have run away: but his enemies held him fast, his enemies were for him one of life's continual seductions, his fury was, just as it was for the ancient Cynics,* his consolation, his refreshment, his compensation, his remedy against disgust, his *happiness*. So much for the most personal aspect of Schopenhauer's case. On the other hand, there is something typical about it—and only now we return to our problem. As long as philosophers have existed on earth, regardless of their location (from India to England, to take the opposite poles of the talent for philosophy), there is no disputing the fact that they have harboured feelings of irritation and rancour towards sensuality—Schopenhauer is only their most eloquent and, if one has the ears to hear it, also their most exciting and delightful spokesman. Likewise there exists among philosophers a real bias and warmth in favour of the entire ascetic ideal, one should have no illusions about that. Both belong, as I said, to the type; if both are lacking in a philosopher, then he will never be anything more than a 'so-called' philosopher—one may be sure of that. What is the *meaning* of this? For this state of affairs requires interpretation: *in themselves*, the facts stand there, mute to all eternity, like all 'things in themselves'. All animals, including *la bête philosophe*,* strive instinctively for an optimum combination of favourable conditions which allow them to expend all their energy and achieve their maximum feeling of power; equally instinctively, and with a fine sense of smell which is 'higher than any reason', all animals loathe any kind of trouble-maker or obstacle which either actually obstructs their path to this optimum combination or has the potential to do so (—I am *not* talking here about their path to happiness, but their path to power, to action, to the most powerful action, which is in most cases actually the path to unhappiness). In the same way, the philosopher loathes marriage along with all the arguments in its favour—marriage as obstacle and disaster on the path to the optimum. Which of the great philosophers up to now has been married? Heraclitus, Plato, Descartes, Spinoza, Leibniz, Kant, Schopenhauer—none of them married; further, it is impossible even to *imagine* them married. A married philosopher belongs *in comedy*, such is my proposition: and that exception Socrates—the mischievous Socrates, it seems, got married *ironice*,* expressly in order to prove this very proposition. All philosophers would say, as Buddha once said when the birth of a son was reported to him: 'Rahula* has been born to me, a chain has been forged for me' (Rahula here means 'a small demon'). A contemplative hour must come to every 'free spirit'—assuming that he previously had a thoughtless hour—as it once came to Buddha—'Domestic life' he thought to himself, 'is narrow and constrained, the house a place of impurity; freedom lies in abandoning the house': 'as he thought this, he abandoned the house'. The ascetic ideal points the way to so many bridges to *independence* that a philosopher cannot refrain from rejoicing inwardly and clapping his hands when he hears the story of all those who have made up their minds and one day said No to all constraints on freedom and gone forth into some *desert* or other: even assuming that they were merely strong asses and the very antithesis of a strong spirit. In this light, what is the meaning of the ascetic ideal for a philosopher? My answer is—as will be clear by now: in beholding the ascetic ideal, the philosopher sees before him the optimum conditions for the highest and boldest spirituality, and smiles—in the process, he does *not* deny 'existence', but rather affirms his *own* existence and *nothing but* his own existence, and this perhaps to the extent that he is not far from the sinful wish: *pereat mundus, fiat philosophia, fiat philosophus*, **fiam**!...*

8

Clearly, these philosophers are far from impartial witnesses and judges of the *value* of the ascetic ideal! They are thinking of *themselves*—what is the 'saint' to them! They are thinking of what is most indispensable to *them*: freedom from compulsion, disturbance, noise, business, duties, worries: clear-headedness; the dance, leap, and flight of thought; good air, thin, clear, free, dry, like air at altitude, in which all animal being becomes more spiritual and grows wings; all underground cellars silent; all dogs nicely on a leash; no hostile barking and shaggy rancour; no gnawing worms of injured ambition; modest and submissive intestines, diligent as mills, but distant; the heart remote, beyond, pregnant with the future, posthumous. All in all, when they think of the ascetic ideal what comes to mind is the happy asceticism of a deified and fully fledged animal, an animal which does not so much remain at rest as hover over life. The three splendid slogans of the ascetic ideal are well known: poverty, humility, chastity. Now take a close look at the life of all great, fruitful, inventive spirits—you will always find all three present to some extent. But absolutely *not*, as goes without saying, as if these were 'virtues'—what are virtues to this kind of man!—, rather as the most authentic and most natural conditions of their *optimum* existence, their *most beautiful* fruitfulness. In order to achieve this, their domineering spirituality was very probably forced to bridle an unrestrained and irritable pride or a wilful sensuality, or perhaps struggled to maintain the will to the 'desert' against an inclination to the choice and luxurious, not to mention against a profligate generosity of hand and heart. But this domineering spirituality succeeded, being, as it was, the domineering instinct which asserted its demands over all the other instincts,—and it continues to do so; if it did not, it would simply cease to dominate. So there is no question of 'virtue' here. By the way, the *desert* of which I just spoke, where spirits of strong and independent constitution withdraw in isolation—oh, how different it looks from the desert imagined by intellectuals!—, for in some cases, these intellectuals are themselves the desert. And there is no doubt that all those who play the part of spiritual men would simply be unable to endure it—it is not Romantic and Syrian enough, not nearly enough of a theatrical desert! Certainly, there is no shortage of camels: but there any resemblance ends. A willed obscurity, perhaps; an avoidance of the self; a timidity in the face of commotion, honour, the press, influence; a modest official function, a routine, something which offers concealment rather than exposure to the light; occasionally, the refreshing sight of harmless, happy animals and birds; a mountain landscape for company, but not a dead one, rather one with *eyes* (that is, with lakes); possibly even a room in a busy, run-of-the-mill guest-house, where one can be confident of going unrecognized and talk to everyone with impunity—that is what 'desert' means here: oh, it is lonely enough, believe me!* When Heraclitus withdrew into the courtyards and colonnades of the great Temple of Artemis,* his was a worthier 'desert', I admit: why do we have no such temples? (—perhaps we *do* have them: I am thinking now of my most beautiful study, the *piazza di San Marco*,* in spring, of course, between ten and twelve in the morning). But what Heraclitus avoided is no different from what *we* continue to avoid today: commotion and the democratic chatter of the Ephesians, their politics, their news of the 'Empire'* (the Persian Empire, you understand), the trash of the market-place, of 'the contemporary'—for we philosophers need respite principally from *one* thing: from 'the contemporary', above all. We respect silence, coolness, refinement, distance, the past, anything in the main which does not force the soul to defend and constrict itself—something with which one may converse quietly and unobserved. Just listen to the sound made by a spirit when it talks: every spirit has its sound, loves its sound. This one here, for example, must be an agitator, I mean an empty head, an empty vessel; whatever goes in comes out muffled and thick, weighed down with the echo of a great void. That one there seldom speaks but with a hoarse voice: has he perhaps *thought* himself hoarse? Such a thing would in principle be possible—ask the physiologists. But whoever thinks in *words*, thinks as an orator and not as a thinker (this reveals basically that he is not thinking in facts, is not thinking factually, but only with reference to facts, that what he is actually thinking about is himself and his audience). This third one here talks insistently, his presence is physically intrusive, his breath wafts over us—we shut our mouths involuntarily, although he is speaking to us through a book. The sound of his style explains all this—he is short of time, he lacks self-confidence, he will have his say now or never again. But a self-assured spirit speaks softly; it seeks seclusion, it keeps people waiting. A philosopher may be identified by the fact that he avoids three glittering and noisy things—fame, princes, and women: which is not to say that they may not come to him. He shies away from light which is all too bright: for that reason he shies away from his time and its 'daylight'. In his day, he is like a shadow: the deeper the sun sinks, the greater he becomes. As far as his 'humility' is concerned, he endures a certain dependence and obscurity, just as he endures the darkness: even more, he is afraid of being disturbed by lightning, he recoils in fright from the exposure of an all-too isolated and abandoned tree, its vulnerability to every moody storm and every stormy mood. His 'maternal' instinct, his secret love for what is growing within him, leads him to places where he is relieved of thinking about *himself*; in the same way as the instinctive *mother* in woman has up to now for the most part maintained her in a position of dependence. Ultimately, they make few enough demands, these philosophers, their motto is: 'He who possesses is possessed'—: *not*, as I am obliged to keep repeating, out of virtue, out of a meritorious will to self-sufficiency and simplicity, but rather because their highest master demands this of them, in his wisdom and ruthlessness; their master with his sense for one thing only, accumulating and storing up everything—time, strength, love, interest—only for that. This kind of man dislikes being disturbed by enmities or friendships; he forgets or despises with equal ease. He deems it in bad taste to play the martyr; 'to *suffer* for the truth'—he leaves that to the ambitious men and the stage heroes of the spirit and whoever else has the time for it (—the philosophers, on the other hand, are obliged to *do* something for the truth). They are sparing in their use of big words; they are even said to have an aversion to the word 'truth': it sounds boastful... Finally, as far as the 'chastity' of the philosophers is concerned, the fertility of this kind of spirit is clearly to be sought elsewhere than in children; as is, perhaps, the survival of their name, their small share of immortality (among philosophers in ancient India an even less modest expression was current: 'Of what use are descendants to him whose soul is the world?'). There is no question here of chastity resulting from ascetic scruple or hatred of the senses, just as little as when an athlete or a jockey abstains from women: this is rather the will of their domineering instinct, at least in times of the great pregnancy. Every artist knows how harmful the effects of sexual intercourse are when in a condition of great spiritual tension and preparation; for the most powerful artists, those with the surest instincts, the primary factor here is not experience, bad experience—but rather their 'maternal' instinct, which in the interests of the gestating work ruthlessly assumes control of all the other reserves and accumulations of strength, of the *vigor** of animal life: the greater strength then *consumes* the smaller.—Let us then explicate the aforementioned case of Schopenhauer in the light of this interpretation: there, the sight of the beautiful obviously operated as a catalytic stimulus to the *principal strength* of his nature (the strength of contemplation and of profound perspicacity); in such a way that the latter then exploded and all at once came to dominate his consciousness. This is not at all to exclude the possibility that the peculiar sweetness and plenitude which characterizes the aesthetic condition might originate in an element of 'sensuality' (just as the 'idealism' which characterizes sexually mature girls springs from the same source)—sensuality is not cancelled out* through the onset of the aesthetic condition, as Schopenhauer believed, but only transfigured and no longer present to consciousness as a sexual stimulus.* (I will return to this point of view on another occasion, in connection with the even more delicate problems of the *physiology of aesthetics*,* a field which has so far remained completely untouched and unexplored.)

9

As we have seen, a certain asceticism, a severe and serene abstemiousness of the best intentions will be numbered among the conditions which are conducive to the highest spirituality, as well as to its most natural consequences: so it will from now on come as no surprise to learn that philosophers have always been favourably biased in their treatment of the ascetic ideal. A serious historical investigation reveals that the link between the ascetic ideal and philosophy is even closer and stronger. It might be said that it was only at the *apron-strings* of this ideal that philosophy learnt to take its first steps, its very first short steps on earth—oh, still so clumsy, oh, with such a morose expression, oh, so ready to tumble over and lie on its stomach, this shy and delicate toddler with bandy legs! Philosophy began as all good things do—for a long time it lacked confidence in itself, it looked around constantly to see if someone would come to its aid, even more, it was afraid of everyone who looked its way. Draw up a list of the individual drives and virtues of the philosopher—his drive to doubt, his drive to negate, his drive to wait (his 'ephectic'* drive), his drive to analyse, his drive to research, to seek, to dare, his drive to compare, to balance, his will to neutrality and objectivity, his will to all '*sine ira et studio*'*—: has one even begun to appreciate how, throughout most of their existence, all these drives were in contradiction with the elementary demands of morality and conscience? (not to mention those of *reason* above all, which even Luther liked to call 'Mistress Clever, the clever whore'). That a philosopher, *had* he attained consciousness, would necessarily have felt himself to be the embodiment of the '*nitimur in vetitum*'*—and consequently took care *not* to 'feel himself', *not* to attain consciousness?... As I said, this is no different from all the good things in which we take pride today; even if measured according to the criteria of the ancient Greeks, our whole modern being, in so far as it is not weakness but power and consciousness of power, continues to distinguish itself as sheer hubris* and godlessness: for throughout most of history it has been the very opposite of the things we honour today which have had conscience on their side and God as their guardian. Today our whole attitude towards nature is one of hubris, our violation of nature with the aid of machines and the thoughtless ingenuity of technicians and engineers. Our attitude towards God is one of hubris, by that I mean our attitude towards some spider of finality and morality which is supposed to exist behind the great net and web of causality—we might say as Charles the Bold did in his struggle with Louis XI, '*je combats l'universelle araignée*'.* Our attitude towards ourselves is one of hubris, for we experiment with ourselves in a way which we would never allow ourselves to experiment with any animal, we derive pleasure from our curious dissection of the soul of a living body. What is the 'salvation' of the soul to us! We will heal ourselves later: sickness is instructive, we have no doubt, even more instructive than health—*those who cause sickness* today appear even more indispensable to us than any medicine-men and 'saviours'. Now we violate even ourselves, there is no doubt, we nutcrackers of the soul, both questioning and questionable, as if nut-cracking were all there were to life; and in the process we must necessarily become more questionable by the day, increasingly *worthy* of asking questions, in the process perhaps even worthier—of life?... All good things were previously bad things, every original sin has been transformed into an original virtue. Marriage, for example, long appeared a sin against the rights of the community; at one time one did penance for being so immodest and so presumptuous as to take a woman for oneself (to this belonged, for example, the *jus primae noctis*,* which remains even today the prerogative of priests in Cambodia, those guardians of the 'good old ways'). The gentle, benevolent, compliant, compassionate feelings—so highly valued as to be practically the 'values as such'—were throughout most of history the object of self-contempt: one felt ashamed of one's mildness, as today one feels ashamed of one's harshness (compare *Beyond Good and Evil*, §260). Subordination to the *law*:—oh, how the consciences of the noble races the earth over were loath to renounce the *vendetta** and submit to the authority of the law! For a long time, the 'law' was a *vetitum*,* a sin, an innovation, it appeared on the scene with violence, in the *form* of violence, to which one submitted only in shame before oneself. Spiritual and physical torture has been the price paid for even the smallest step on earth: this whole perspective, 'that not only the step forward, no! but every single step, movement, change has required countless martyrs', sounds so strange to us, especially today—I brought this to light in *Daybreak* (§18). 'Nothing is more dearly bought', so it goes there, 'than the small amount of human reason and sense of freedom which is our pride today. But it is because of this pride that today we find it almost impossible to identify with those extended periods of the "morality of custom" which preceded "world history", that really decisive fundamental history which established the character of mankind: those periods when suffering, cruelty, distortion, revenge, denial of reason were regarded as virtues, while comfort, curiosity, peace and compassion were regarded as dangers, and work and the sympathy of others were regarded as insults, madness regarded as divine, *change* as immorality and the seed of disaster!'—

10

In the same book (§42), I set out the kind of evaluation, the *pressure* of evaluation under which the most ancient race of contemplative men had to live—despised in exact measure as it was incapable of inspiring fear! Contemplation first appeared on earth in disguise, it looked ambiguous, with an evil heart and often wearing a frightened expression: about that there is no doubt. For a long time, the inactive, brooding, and unwarlike character of the instincts of contemplative men aroused deep mistrust all around: there was no other means against this than the determination to inspire *fear* of oneself. The old Brahmin, for example, knew how to set about that! The most ancient philosophers were able to give their existence and appearance a meaning, a support, an underlying reason which inculcated *fear* in others. Examined more closely, this derived from an even more fundamental need, that of inspiring self-respect and an inner fear of themselves. For within themselves they found all the value-judgements turned *against* themselves, they had to suppress all sorts of suspicion and resistance towards 'the philosopher within'. As men of a fearful age, they did this with fearful means: self-inflicted cruelty, inventive self-castigation—that was the main instrument of these power-hungry settlers and innovative thinkers who had to violate the gods and tradition in themselves before they could *believe* in their renewal. Remember the famous story of the king Vishvamitra,* who derived such a feeling of power and self-confidence from a thousand years of self-inflicted torture that he undertook the task of building a *new heaven*: the sinister symbol of the most ancient and most recent history of philosophers on earth—anyone who has at some time built a new heaven, drew the power to do so only from his *own hell*... Let us compress this whole state of affairs into a few brief phrases: in order for its existence to be *possible* at all, the philosophical spirit has at first always been obliged to disguise and mask itself in the types of the contemplative man *established in earlier times*, that is, as priest, magician, prophet, above all, as a religious man. For a long time, *the ascetic ideal* has served the philosopher as a form in which to manifest himself, as a pre-condition of existence—he was obliged to *represent* it in order to be a philosopher, and he was obliged to *believe* in it in order to be able to represent it. The particular remoteness of the philosophers—with its negation of the world, its hostility to life, its scepticism towards the senses, its freedom from sensuality—which has survived until very recently, and in the process almost gained currency as *the philosophers' attitude* as such—this is above all a consequence of the critical situation in which philosophy first emerged and managed to endure: that is, in so far as throughout most of history philosophy would not have been *at all possible* on earth without an ascetic shell and disguise, without an ascetic self-misunderstanding. To express this clearly in concrete terms: until very recently the ascetic priest has assumed the dark, repulsive form of a caterpillar, the only form in which philosophy was allowed to live, creeping around... Has this really *changed*? Has the bright and dangerous winged creature, the 'spirit' which this caterpillar concealed within itself, finally, thanks to a sunnier, warmer, brighter world, really sloughed its cocoon and escaped into the light? Is there enough pride, daring, boldness, self-assurance, enough spiritual will, will to responsibility, *freedom of will* available today for 'the philosopher' to be from now on really—*possible* on earth?...

11

Only now, once we have the *ascetic priest* in sight, do we begin to approach our problem—what is the meaning of ascetic ideals?—in all seriousness, only now do things begin to get 'serious': we find ourselves face to face with none other than the *representative of seriousness* itself. 'What is the meaning of "in all seriousness"?'—this even more fundamental question is by this stage perhaps already on our lips: a question for physiologists, of course, but one which we will leave aside for the moment. This ideal constitutes not only the conviction of the ascetic priest, but also his will, his power, his interest. His *right* to exist stands and falls with this ideal: no wonder that we find ourselves confronted with a fearful opponent—assuming, that is, that we do oppose this ideal—such an opponent as fights for his very existence against those who deny the ideal... On the other hand, it is from the outset unlikely that such a personal involvement with our problem would be of particular benefit to the ideal in question; the ascetic priest will be hard pressed to provide the best defence of this ideal—for the same reason that a woman usually fails in her desire to defend 'woman' in general—let alone the most objective commentary and evaluation of the controversy aroused here. Rather than fearing that he will succeed in refuting our case, we will be obliged to help him defend himself successfully against us—that much is already clear... The idea at issue in this struggle is the *value* which the ascetic priests ascribe to our life: they juxtapose this life (along with what belongs to it, 'nature', 'world', the whole sphere of becoming and the ephemeral) to a completely different form of existence, which it opposes and excludes, *unless* it somehow turns itself against itself, *denies itself*. In which case, the case of an ascetic life, life functions as a bridge to that other existence. The ascetic treats life as a wrong track along which one must retrace one's steps to the point at which it begins; or as a mistake which one rectifies through action—indeed, which one *should* rectify: for he *demands* that one should follow him, he imposes wherever he can his *own* evaluation of existence. What does this mean? The inscription of such a monstrous form of evaluation into the history of mankind is neither an exception nor a curiosity: it is one of the most widespread and enduring facts there are. Read from a distant star, perhaps the capitalized script of our existence on earth would lead to the mistaken conclusion that the earth is the distinctively *ascetic star*, a corner full of unhappy, arrogant, and repulsive creatures who are completely incapable of casting off a profound dissatisfaction with themselves, with the earth, with life as a whole, and who cause themselves as much pain as possible, from pleasure in causing pain—probably their sole pleasure. But let us consider how regularly and ubiquitously the ascetic priest appears in almost all periods; he belongs to no single race; he thrives everywhere; he emerges from all classes of society. Not that he somehow breeds and propagates his mode of evaluation through heredity—rather, generally speaking, a profound instinct prevents him from reproducing. It can only be a necessity of the first order which allows this species to grow and flourish in spite of its *hostility to life*—it must somehow be in the *interest of life itself* that such a self-contradictory type does not die out. For an ascetic life is a contradiction in terms: a particular kind of *ressentiment* rules there, that of an unsatisfied instinct and will to power which seeks not to master some isolated aspect of life but rather life itself, its deepest, strongest, most fundamental conditions; an attempt is made to use strength to dam up the very source of strength; a green and cunning gaze is directed against thriving physiological growth, especially against its expression, beauty, joy; while a pleasure is felt and *sought* in failure, atrophy, pain, accident, ugliness, arbitrary atonements, self-denial, self-flagellation, self-sacrifice. All this is paradoxical to an extreme: we find ourselves confronted here with a contradiction which wills itself as a contradiction, which derives *enjoyment* from this suffering and even becomes increasingly self-assured and triumphant in proportion as its own pre-condition, the physiological capacity for life, *diminishes*. 'Triumph at the very moment of ultimate agony': the ascetic ideal has from its earliest days fought under this superlative sign; in this seductive enigma, in this image of delight and suffering, it recognized its brightest light, its salvation, its final victory. *Crux, nux, lux**—in the ascetic ideal they are as one.—

12

Assuming that such an incarnate will to contradiction and the unnatural can be brought to *philosophize*: upon what will it indulge its innermost whim? Upon what is felt with the greatest certainty to be true, to be real: it will seek *error* in the very place where the authentic instinct of life most unconditionally posits truth. It will, for example, reduce the physical world to an illusion, as the ascetics of Vedanta* philosophy did, along with pain, diversity, the whole conceptual opposition of 'subject' and 'object'*—errors, nothing but errors! To cease believing in one's own self, to deny one's own 'reality'—what a triumph!—no longer merely over the senses, over appearance, but a much higher kind of triumph, a cruel violation of *reason*:

a lasciviousness which reaches its peak when ascetic self-contempt, the self-mockery of reason decrees: 'A realm of truth and freedom *does exist*, but reason is the very thing which is excluded from it!'... (Incidentally: something of this lascivious contradictoriness of asceticism, with its love of turning reason against reason, persists even in the Kantian concept of the 'intelligible character of things':* for according to Kant, 'intelligible character' means that things are constituted in such a way that they are understood only to the extent that the intellect acknowledges them as *completely beyond its grasp*.)— But ultimately, and particularly in our capacity as seekers after knowledge, let us be duly grateful for such resolute reversals of the usual perspectives and evaluations, by means of which the spirit has for all too long raged against itself in an apparently sinful and senseless way: to see differently, the *desire* to see differently for once in this way is no small discipline of the intellect and a preparation for its eventual 'objectivity'—this latter understood not as 'disinterested contemplation' (which is a non-concept and a nonsense), but as the capacity to have all the arguments for and against *at one's disposal* and to suspend or implement them at will: so that one can exploit that very *diversity* of perspectives and affective interpretations in the interests of knowledge. From now on, my dear philosophers, let us beware of the dangerous old conceptual fable which posited a 'pure, will-less, painless, timeless knowing subject', let us beware of the tentacles of such contradictory concepts as 'pure reason', 'absolute spirituality', 'knowledge in itself';—for these always ask us to imagine an eye which is impossible to imagine, an eye which supposedly looks out in no particular direction, an eye which supposedly either restrains or altogether lacks the active powers of interpretation which first make seeing into seeing something—for here, then, a nonsense and non-concept is demanded of the eye. Perspectival seeing is the *only* kind of seeing there is, perspectival 'knowing' the *only* kind of 'knowing'; and the *more* feelings about a matter which we allow to come to expression, the *more* eyes, different eyes through which we are able to view this same matter, the more complete our 'conception' of it, our 'objectivity', will be. But to eliminate the will completely, to suspend the feelings altogether, even assuming that we could do so: what? would this not amount to the *castration* of the intellect?...

13

But let us return to our problem. It is clear from the outset that such a self-contradiction as the ascetic priest seems to represent, that of 'life against life', is, in terms of physiology now rather than psychology, simply nonsense. It can be nothing more than *apparent*; it must be a kind of provisional expression, an interpretation, a formula, a disguise, a psychological misunderstanding of something whose real nature could not be understood and identified for *what it really was*—a mere word, lodged in an old *gap* in human understanding. To contrast this briefly with the actual facts of the matter: *the ascetic ideal is derived from the protective and healing instincts of a degenerating life*, which seeks to preserve itself and fights for existence with any available means; it points to a partial physiological inhibition and fatigue against which those deepest instincts of life which have remained intact struggle incessantly with new means and inventions. The ascetic ideal is such a means: the situation is thus the very opposite of what those who revere this ideal think—in it and through it, life struggles with death and *against* death, the ascetic ideal is a trick played in order to *preserve* life. That this ideal was able to attain power and dominate men to the extent which history demonstrates, particularly wherever the civilization and taming of man was set under way, is the expression of a great fact: the *sickliness* of the type of man which has existed so far, of the tamed man at least, of this man's physiological struggle against death (more precisely: against disgust with life, against exhaustion, against the desire for the 'end'). The ascetic priest embodies the desire for another existence, somewhere else, is even the highest form of this desire, its real intensity and passion. But the very *power* of this desire is the chain which binds him to this life; this very power transforms him into an instrument, obliged to work to create more favourable conditions for human life as it exists here—by means of this very *power* he sustains securely in life the whole herd of failures, the disaffected, the underprivileged, the victims, all those kinds of people who suffer from themselves, and he does so by instinctively walking ahead of them as a shepherd. My point is already clear: this ascetic priest, this apparent enemy of life, this *man of negation*—yes, even he counts among the very great forces which *conserve* and *affirm* life... What is the reason for this sickliness? For man is more sick, more uncertain, more mutable, less defined than any other animal, there is no doubt about that—he is *the* sick animal: why is that? Certainly, he has also been more daring, innovative, and defiant and has challenged fate more than all the other animals put together: he, the great experimenter with himself, the unsatisfied, unsated one who struggles with animal, nature, and the gods for ultimate mastery—he, the one who remains undefeated, eternally oriented towards the future, who can find no respite from his own compelling energy, so that the spur of the future mercilessly digs into the skin of every present—how should such a courageous and well-endowed animal not also be the most endangered, the most chronically and deeply sick of all the sick animals?... Man has had enough—there are, often enough, whole epidemics of this satiety (—thus around 1348, at the time of the dance of death); but, like everything else, even this disgust, this fatigue, this frustration with himself emerges so powerfully in him that it is immediately transformed into another chain. The No which he says to life brings, as if by magic, an abundance of tender Yeses to light; even when this master of destruction, of self-destruction *wounds* himself—it is the wound itself which afterwards compels him to *live*...

14

The more normal sickliness is in man—and we cannot dispute its normality—the more one should repect the rare cases of psychic and physical strength, mankind's *strokes of luck*, and all the more carefully protect those who are well constituted from the worst air, the air of the sick. Is this what we do?... The sick represent the greatest danger for the healthy; it is *not* the strongest but the weakest who spell disaster for the strong. Do we appreciate this?... Broadly speaking, it is not fear of man which one would wish to reduce: for this fear compels the strong to be strong and on occasion fearful—it *maintains* the well-constituted type of man. What is to be feared, as having an incomparably disastrous effect, would not be great fear of man, but great *disgust*; as well as great *compassion*. If these two were ever to mate, their union would inevitably and immediately bring forth something most sinister into the world, the 'last will' of man, his will to nothingness, nihilism. And indeed: in many ways, the time is ripe for this. Anyone whose sense of smell extends beyond his nose to his eyes and ears detects almost everywhere he goes something like the air of the asylum, the hospital—I am talking, admittedly, of the cultural domains of man, of every kind of 'Europe' which still exists on earth. The *sickly* constitute the greatest danger to man: *not* the evil, *not* the 'predators'. Those who are from the outset victims, downtrodden, broken—they are the ones, the *weakest* are the ones who most undermine life among men, who most dangerously poison and question our trust in life, in man. Where might one escape this veiled look, which leaves one with a deep feeling of sorrow as one walks away, that introspective look of the man deformed from the outset, a look which reveals the way in which such a man speaks to himself—that gaze which is a sigh! 'I wish I were anyone else but myself!' this gaze sighs: 'but there is no hope of that. I am who I am: how could I escape from myself? And yet—*I have had enough of myself*!'... On such a ground of self-contempt, a real quagmire, every weed will grow, every poisonous plant, and all so tiny, so hidden, so dishonest, so sweet. Here the worms of vindictive feeling and reaction squirm; here the air stinks of things kept secret and unacknowledged; here the net of malicious conspiracy is continually spun—the conspiracy of the suffering against the well-constituted and the victorious, here the sight of the victor is the object of *hatred*. And what deceitfulness is required in order not to acknowledge this hatred as hatred! What an expenditure of grand words and gestures, what an art of 'honest' defamation! These failures: what noble eloquence streams from their lips! How their eyes swim with so much sugary, slimy, humble devotion! What are they really after? To *represent*, at least, justice, love, wisdom, superiority—such is the ambition of these 'lowest of the low', these sick men! And how skilful such an ambition makes them! Admire in particular the forger's skill with which the stamp, even the jangle, the golden sound of virtue is faked here. They monopolize virtue now, these weak and incurably sick men, there is no doubt about that: 'We alone are the good, the just', this is the way they speak, 'we alone are the *homines bonae voluntatis*.'* They wander around among us as living reproaches and warnings—as if health, good constitution, strength, pride, the sense of power were in themselves marks of depravity, which would at some stage require atonement, bitter atonement: ah, how ready they are at bottom to *compel* atonement, how they thirst after the opportunity to be *executioners*. There is among them a plethora of vindictive men disguised as judges, whose mouths continually secrete the word 'justice' like a poisonous saliva, with lips always pursed, ready to spit at anything which looks content and goes its way in good spirits. Among them too there is no shortage of that most revolting species of vain men, the deceitful deformities who are out to play the part of 'beautiful souls',* and to hawk around their ruined sensuality, dressed up in poetry and other swaddling clothes, as 'purity of heart': the species of moral onanists and those who indulge in 'self-satisfaction'. The will of the sick to display *any* form of superiority, its instinct for secret paths which lead to a tyranny over the healthy—where is it not to be found, this will to power of the weakest! The sick woman in particular: her techniques of domination, compulsion, and tyranny are unsurpassed in their refinement. To that end, the sick woman spares nothing living, nothing dead, she disinters the most deeply buried things (the Bogos* say: 'Woman is a hyena'). Look behind the scenes of every family, every organization, every community: the struggle of the sick against the healthy is everywhere to be found—a silent struggle for the most part, with poison in small doses, with pinpricks, with sly games of long-suffering expressions, but also with that Pharisee* tactic of the sick, the *loud* gesture, whose favourite part is that of 'righteous indignation'. It would like to make itself heard even upon the consecrated ground of science, this hoarse indignant bark of the sickly dog, the biting, rabid deceit of such 'righteous' Pharisees (—I remind readers who have ears to hear once again of that apostle of revenge from Berlin, Eugen Dühring, who is making the most indecent and repulsive use of moral mumbo-jumbo in Germany today: Dühring, the foremost moral bigmouth around at the moment, even among his kind, the anti-Semites). They are all men of *ressentiment*, these deformed and maggot-ridden men, a whole tremulous realm of subterranean revenge, inexhaustible, insatiable in its outbursts against the fortunate and also in masquerades of revenge, in pretexts for revenge: at what point would they really attain their ultimate, finest, most sublime triumph of revenge? Without doubt, once they succeeded in forcing their own misery, the whole of misery as such *into the conscience* of the fortunate: so that these latter would one day begin to feel ashamed of their good fortune and perhaps say to one another: 'It is a disgrace to be fortunate! *there is too much misery!*'... But there could be no greater or more disastrous misunderstanding than when the fortunate, the well constituted, the powerful in body and soul begin to doubt their *right to good fortune* in this way. Away with this 'world turned upside-down'! Away with this shameful weakening of sensibility! That the sick should *not* infect the healthy with their sickness—which is what such a weakening would represent—this ought to be the prime concern on earth—but that requires above all that the healthy should remain *segregated* from the sick, protected even from the sight of the sick, so that they do not mistake themselves for the sick. Or would it somehow be their mission to act as orderlies and physicians?... But they could not mistake and deny *their* mission in a worse way—the higher *should* not reduce itself to an instrument of the lower, the pathos of distance* *should* keep even their missions separate to all eternity! Their right to exist, the prerogative of the bell with a full tone over the one which is cracked and out of tune, is a thousand times greater: they alone are the *guarantors* of the future, they alone are *under an obligation* to the future of mankind. The sick would never be allowed to do what *they* can and must do: but *if* they are to be able to do what *they* alone should do, how could the possibility of acting as physician, as bringer of consolation, as 'saviour' of the sick remain open to them?... So may we have good air! good air! and away in any case from the vicinity of all asylums and hospitals of culture! So may we have good company, *our* company! Or isolation, if necessary! But away in any case from the foul smell of inner corruption and the secret worm-fodder of the sick!... So that we ourselves especially, my friends, may defend ourselves at least for a little while longer against the two worst plagues which could have been reserved for us in particular—against *great disgust at man!* against *great compassion for man!*...

15

If one has grasped in all profundity—and here especially I insist on a *profound grasp*, a profound understanding—how it simply *cannot* be the mission of the healthy to wait on the sick, to heal the sick, then one has understood one further necessity—the necessity for physicians and nurses *who are themselves sick*: and here we hold in both hands the meaning of the ascetic priest. We must regard the ascetic priest as the predestined saviour, shepherd, and advocate of the sick herd: only then do we begin to understand his tremendous historical mission. The *dominion of the suffering* is his realm, his instinct points him in that direction, there he finds his most authentic art, his mastery, his kind of good fortune. He must himself be sick, he must be fundamentally related to the sick and underprivileged in order to understand them—in order to come to an understanding with them; but he must also be strong, even more a master of himself than of others, with his will to power virtually unscathed, so that he inspires the trust and fear of the sick, so that he can be for them a support, resistance, aid, compulsion, prison-master, tyrant, god. He has to defend his herd—against whom? Against the healthy, of course, but also against envy of the healthy; he must be the natural opponent *and despiser* of all raw, stormy, unrestrained, hard, violent, predatory health and power. The priest is the prototype of the *more delicate* animal to which contempt comes more easily than hatred. He will be obliged to lead a war against the predators, a war of cunning (of the 'spirit') more than violence, as goes without saying—to this end, he may possibly have to develop, or at least *represent*, a new form of the predatory type in himself—a new animal ferocity, in which the polar bear, the supple, cold, and patient tiger, and not least the fox appear bound together in a unity as attractive as it is terrifying. If left with no other choice, he may then emerge among the other kind of predators with bearish seriousness, venerable, wise, cold, deceptively superior, as the vanguard and spokesman of more secret forces, intent on sowing pain, self-division, self-contradiction wherever he can, and only too sure of his skill in mastering *those who suffer* at all times. He brings salves and balsam, there is no doubt; but he needs to wound before he can cure; then, in relieving the pain he has inflicted, *he poisons the wound*—for this is his particular area of expertise, this magician and tamer of predators, in whose circle everything healthy necessarily falls sick and everything sick is tamed. In fact, this strange shepherd defends his sick herd well enough—he defends them against themselves too, against the baseness, spite, malice, and whatever else is particular to all addicts and sick men and which smoulders in the herd itself. He engages his cunning in a tough and secret struggle against the anarchy of the herd, the continual threat of its disintegration, the herd in which that most dangerous explosive substance, *ressentiment*, is piled ever higher. To discharge this explosive in such a way as to avoid blowing up either the herd or the shepherd is his greatest master-stroke, and also his supreme usefulness. If one wanted to sum up the value of the priestly existence as succinctly as possible, one might say straight away: the priest *changes the direction* of *ressentiment*. For every suffering man instinctively seeks a cause for his suffering; more precisely, a doer, more definitely, a *guilty* doer, someone capable of suffering—in short, something living on which he can upon any pretext discharge his feelings either in fact or *in effigie*:* for the discharge of feelings represents the greatest attempt on the part of the suffering man to find relief, *anaesthetic*, his involuntarily desired narcotic against pain of any sort. According to my hypothesis, it is here alone, in a desire to *anaesthetize pain through feeling*, that the real physiological cause of *ressentiment*, of revenge, and related matters is to be found—although generally this is sought, quite wrongly it seems to me, in the defensive counter-strike, a merely reactive protective measure, a 'reflex movement' in the case of any kind of sudden injury and danger, like the way in which a frog still seeks to escape a corrosive acid once decapitated. But the difference is fundamental here: in one instance, the desire is to prevent further injury, in the other, to *anaesthetize* by means of any more intense emotion a secret pain and torment which is becoming unbearable, and so to exclude it from consciousness for a moment at least. And for this purpose a feeling is required, the most intense feeling possible, and, in order to stimulate it, the first pretext which happens along. 'Someone must be to blame for the fact that I do not feel well'—this kind of reasoning is characteristic of all sickly people, and all the more so the more the true cause of their not feeling well, the physiological one, remains hidden (—it may lie in a sickening of the *nervus sympathicus** or in excessive secretion from the gall-bladder, in a deficiency of sulphuric or phosphoric potash in the blood, or in poor circulation in the lower body, or in the degeneration of the ovaries or the like). The suffering are gifted with a horrific readiness and inventiveness in finding pretexts for painful feelings; they even enjoy being suspicious, grumbling over misdeeds and apparent insults, they rummage through the entrails of their past and present in search of dark, questionable stories which allow them to revel in a painful mistrust and to intoxicate themselves on their own malicious poison—they tear open the oldest wounds, they bleed from scars long healed, they make evil-doers out of friends, wives, children, and whatever else is closest to them. 'I am suffering: someone must be to blame'—this is how all sickly sheep think. But their shepherd, the ascetic priest, tells them: 'Just so, my sheep! someone must be to blame: but you yourself are this someone, you alone are to blame—*you alone are to blame for yourself!*'... That is bold enough, false enough: but one thing at least is achieved in the process—through this, as I said, the direction of *ressentiment* is—*changed*.

16

From this point on one is in a position to guess what, in my view, the healing instinct of life has at least *attempted* through the figure of the ascetic priest, and what end was served by a provisional tyranny of such paradoxical and paralogical concepts as 'guilt', 'sin', 'sinfulness', 'depravity', 'damnation': that of rendering the sick to a certain extent *harmless*, of destroying the incurable through themselves, of giving the less seriously ill a strict orientation towards themselves, an introspective turn to their *ressentiment* ('One thing is needful'—*) and in such a way to *exploit* the bad instincts of all the suffering to the end of self-discipline, self-surveillance, self-overcoming. As goes without saying, in the case of 'medication' of this kind, a sheerly emotional medication, there is simply no question of a real *healing* of the sick in the physiological sense; it would be out of place even to suggest that such a cure was what the life-instinct somehow expected and intended. On the one hand, a kind of concentration and organization of the sick (—the word 'church' is the most popular term for this); on the other hand, a kind of provisional consolidation of the position of those with healthier constitutions, those more fully formed, and in the process the tearing open of an *abyss* between the healthy and the sick—for a long time this was all that was intended! And it was a great deal! it was a *very great deal*!... (In this essay, as one sees, I proceed from an assumption which, with respect to the kind of readers I require, I need not justify: that man's 'sinfulness' is not an established set of facts, but rather only the interpretation of a set of facts, that is, of physiological distemper—this latter seen from the perspective of morality and religion, which is no longer binding for us.—The fact that someone *feels* 'guilty' or 'sinful' simply does not prove that he is right to do so; no more than that someone is healthy merely because he feels healthy. Remember the famous witch-trials:* at that time even the most perceptive and humane judges had no doubt as to the guilt of the accused; even the 'witches' *themselves had no doubt*—and yet there was no guilt.—To give a more general expression to this assumption: in my view, 'spiritual suffering' itself is far from being a fact, but counts only as an interpretation [causal interpretation]* of sets of facts which have so far resisted precise formulation: as something which continues to float vaguely in the air without any claim to the status of science—really a fat word in place of what is only a question-mark, and a spindly one at that. If someone cannot deal with 'spiritual suffering', then, to put it crudely, this is not the fault of his 'spirit'; but more probably that of his stomach [to put it crudely, as I said: which in no way expresses the desire to be heard crudely, to be understood crudely...]. A stronger man with a better constitution digests his experiences [deeds, misdeeds included], as he digests his meals, even when the food is tough. If he cannot 'deal' with an experience, then this kind of indigestion is as much a matter of physiology as the other kind—and is in fact often only one of the consequences of the other kind.—Between ourselves, it is possible to hold such a view and remain the strictest opponent of all materialism*...)

17

But is he really a *physician*, this ascetic priest?—We have already seen why it is scarcely permissible to call him a physician, however much he might like to feel himself a 'saviour' and be revered as such. He combats only suffering itself, the listlessness of the suffering man, and *not* their cause, *not* the real sickness—this must be our most fundamental objection to the priestly medication. But if one adopts for once the only perspective known to the priest, then one will scarcely be able to restrain one's admiration for all that he saw, sought, and found through it. The *alleviation* of suffering, 'consolation' of all kinds—this is revealed as his distinctive genius; with what inventiveness he has understood his mission of consolation, how boldly and unhesitatingly he has chosen the means to it! Christianity in particular might be called a great treasure-house of the most ingenious consolations; it has stored up so much that is refreshing, soothing, and anaesthetizing; it has run such dangerous and daring risks to this end; it has demonstrated such Mediterranean refinement in its evaluation of which kinds of emotional stimuli have the ability to overcome, at least for a time, the deep depression, leaden fatigue and black sadness of those who are physiologically inhibited. To generalize: the prime concern of all great religions is the struggle against a certain fatigue and inertia which has grown to epidemic proportions. One may assume in advance the probability that a *feeling of physiological inhibition* periodically comes to dominate the broad masses in particular parts of the world, a feeling which, through lack of physiological knowledge, does not appear as such to the conscious mind, with the result that its 'cause' and remedy can only be sought and attempted through psychology and morality (—this is my most general formula for what is commonly called a '*religion*'). Such a feeling of physiological inhibition may derive from several sources: for instance, from the miscegenation of two races which are too far removed from one another (or of two classes—classes too always express differences of race and origin: European 'Weltschmerz',* the 'pessimism' of the nineteenth century is essentially the result of a senselessly sudden mixing of classes); or conditioned through a mistaken emigration—a race arriving in a climate to which it cannot adapt sufficiently (the case of the Indians in India); or the after-effect of the age and fatigue of a race (Parisian pessimism from 1850 on); or the wrong diet (alcoholism in the Middle Ages; the nonsense of *vegetarians**, which, admittedly, has the authority of Shakespeare's foolish knight Sir Andrew Aguecheek* on its side): or from blood-poisoning, malaria, syphilis, and the like (the German depression after the Thirty Years War, which afflicted half of Germany with serious illness and thus prepared the ground for German servility, German faint-heartedness). Such cases represent in each instance a magnificent attempt to *combat the feeling of listlessness*. Let us briefly enumerate its most important practices and forms. (As seems reasonable, I leave aside here the real struggle of the *philosophers* against listlessness, which is usually carried on simultaneously—it is interesting enough, but too absurd, too unconcerned with practicality, too much like a spider's web and the product of idle loafing, as, for instance, when it sets out to prove that pain is an error, naïvely assuming that pain would be *bound* to disappear, once the error is recognized—but look! it refuses to disappear...) *In the first place*, this domineering listlessness is combated through means which reduce the feeling of life itself to its lowest point. Where possible, will and desire are eliminated entirely; everything which produces 'feeling', which produces 'blood' is avoided (a salt-free diet: the hygiene of the fakir); no love; no hatred; equanimity; no revenge; no self-enrichment; no work; begging; where possible, no women, or as few as possible; with respect to the spiritual, Pascal's principle '*il faut s'abêtir*'* is adopted. The result, expressed in terms of psychology and morality, is the 'loss of the self', 'sanctification'; in physiological terms, hypnosis—the attempt to achieve for man something approximating *hibernation* for some kinds of animal, *estivation* for many plants in a hot climate—the minimum metabolic rate which maintains life below the level of real consciousness. A surprising amount of human energy has been expended to this end—has it all been in vain?... There can be no doubt that such sportsmen* of 'sanctity', who flourish at all times and among all peoples, have in fact found a real release from what they used such rigorous training* to combat—in countless cases, their system of hypnosis really helped them to escape from deep physiological depressions: which explains why their methods number among the universal facts of ethnology. There is likewise no justification for counting such an intention to starve the body and its desires as in itself a symptom of madness (as it pleases an awkward kind of beef-eating 'free spirit' and Sir Andrew to). But it certainly points the way to all sorts of mental disturbances, to 'inner lights', for example, as in the case of the Hesychasts of Mount Athos,* to aural and visual hallucinations, to lascivious outpourings and ecstasies of sensuality (the story of St Theresa*). It goes without saying that the interpretation of such states given by those who have undergone them has always been as effusively false as it is possible to be: but we should take care not to miss the tone of conviction and gratitude which rings through even in the *will* to such a type of interpretation. The highest state, *redemption* itself, that finally achieved state of complete hypnosis and silence, continues to be regarded as *the* mystery as such, the mystery which even the highest symbols are inadequate to express, as the return and entry into the ground of things, as liberation from all madness, as 'knowledge', as 'truth', as 'being', as escape from all goals, all desires, all action, as a domain beyond good and evil. 'Good and evil', says the Buddhist, 'are both chains: the Perfect One develops beyond them.'

'What is done and what remains undone', says the believer in the Vedanta, 'causes him no pain; as a wise man, he shakes off good and evil; his domain suffers through no further deed; he goes beyond good and evil, beyond both':—an all-Indian view, then, as Brahmin as it is Buddhist. (Neither in the Indian nor in the Christian way of thinking is it possible to *achieve* this 'redemption' through virtue, through moral improvement, regardless of how high the hypnotic value of virtue is set: one should bear this in mind—the facts corroborate it, as it happens. To have remained *true* on this point may perhaps be regarded as the supreme element of realism in the three great religions, which are otherwise so thoroughly steeped in morality. 'For the seeker after knowledge there is no duty'... 'Redemption cannot be attained through an *increase* in virtue: for it consists in unity with the Brahma, whose perfection is beyond increase; nor can it be obtained through the *removal* of faults: for Brahma, with whom unity constitutes redemption, is eternally pure.' These passages are from the commentary of Shankara, quoted from the work of the first real European *expert* on Indian philosophy, my friend Paul Deussen.*) We ought then to respect the notion of 'redemption' in the great religions. But it will not be easy for us to take seriously the way in which these men who are tired of life, too tired even to dream, appreciate *deep sleep*—deep sleep already envisaged mainly as access to the Brahma, as the *attainment of the unio mystica** with God. 'When he is sound asleep',—so it says in the most ancient and worthy 'scripture'—'and completely at rest, so that he no longer dreams, then he is, oh dearly beloved, united with all that is, he has withdrawn into himself—embraced by the knowledge-like self, he is no longer conscious of what is outside or inside. Neither day nor night, nor age, nor death, nor suffering, nor good nor evil works cross this bridge.' 'In deep sleep', the believers of this most profound of the three great religions likewise say, 'the soul rises up out of the body, enters into the highest light and emerges from it in its own form: there it is the highest spirit itself, which walks around joking and playing and delighting itself, whether with women or with carriages or with friends, then it ceases to think of this appendage of a body, to which the *prâna* (the life-breath) is harnessed like a beast of burden to the cart.' Nevertheless, here too, as in the case of the notion of 'redemption', we should bear in mind that the evaluation expressed here, in however luxurious and exaggerated a manner after the Oriental fashion, is basically no different from that of the clear and cool, Hellenically cool but still suffering Epicurus:* the hypnotic feeling of nothingness, the rest of the deepest sleep, *the absence of pain*, in short—the suffering and fundamentally disgruntled hold this as the highest good, as the value of values, they *must* give it a positive value, feel it to be *the* positive as such. (According to the same logic of feeling, nothingness in all pessimistic religions goes by the name of *God*.)

18

More often than this hypnotic dampening of the capacity for pain and of sensibility as a whole—which already presupposes rare strengths, above all, courage, contempt for opinion, 'intellectual Stoicism'*—a different kind of training* is tried out against states of depression, one which is in any case easier: *mechanical activity*. There is absolutely no doubt that it brings considerable relief to a life of suffering: this state of affairs is nowadays called, somewhat dishonestly, the 'blessing of work'. The relief consists in the fact that the interest of the suffering man is completely distracted from his suffering—that nothing enters into consciousness but activity, continual and repeated activity, and thus leaves little room for suffering: for the chamber of human consciousness is *narrow*! Mechanical activity and all that goes with it—such as absolute regularity, absolute and unconscious obedience, a way of life which has been determined once and for all, time which is fully occupied, a permitted degree of 'impersonality', even a disciplining with a view towards impersonality, towards the forgetting of the self, towards '*incuria sui*'*—: with what subtlety and thoroughness the ascetic priest has known how to use all this in the struggle against suffering! When he had to deal with the suffering of the lower classes in particular, with working slaves or prisoners (or with women: who are for the most part both at the same time, both working slaves and prisoners), it took little more on his part than some ingenuity in changing names, in rebaptizing, in order to make them regard things they had previously loathed as benefits, as pieces of relative good fortune—the slave's dissatisfaction with his fate was *not* in any case invented by the priests.—An even more highly appreciated means in the struggle against depression is the prescription of a *modest pleasure*, something which is readily attainable and can be made available on a regular basis; this medication is often used in conjunction with the one just discussed. Pleasure is prescribed as a remedy most frequently in the form of the pleasure of *giving pleasure* (in the form of good deeds, gifts, relief, help, encouragement, consolation, praise, rewarding); in prescribing 'love of one's neighbour', the ascetic priest is basically prescribing, albeit in the most careful doses, a stimulus for the strongest, most life-affirming drive—the *will to power*. The happiness of 'minimal superiority' which all good deeds, making oneself useful, helping and rewarding bring with them, is the means of consolation which the physiologically inhibited are most accustomed to using and is indeed the most effective, as long as they are well advised: otherwise, they hurt each other, in obedience to the same fundamental instinct, of course. When one looks for the origins of Christianity in the Roman world, one finds organizations of mutual support, associations for the poor, for the sick, for burials, grown up on the humblest ground of the society of that time, organizations in which the chief means against depression, the modest pleasure, that of reciprocal benevolence, was consciously cultivated—perhaps this was something new at that time, a real discovery? Calling forth this 'will to reciprocity', to the formation of a herd, to 'community', to '*cénacle*',* is bound to result in renewed and much more extensive outbreaks of the will to power which it has, even if only slightly, stimulated: the *formation of the herd* marks an essential advance and victory in the struggle against depression. With the growth of the community, a new interest is strengthened even in the individual, and often enough raises him above the most personal aspects of his discontent, his aversion from *himself* (Geulincx's '*despectio sui*'*). From a desire to shake off their stifling listlessness and sense of weakness, all the sick and sickly strive instinctively after a herd organization: the ascetic priest senses this instinct and promotes it; wherever there are herds, it is the instinct of weakness which has willed the herd, and the prudence of priests which has organized it. For the following fact should not be overlooked: the strong are as naturally inclined to *disperse* as the weak are to *congregate*; when the former join together, it is only with a view to an aggressive collective action and satisfaction of their will to power, and with much reluctance on the part of individual conscience; the latter, on the other hand, take pleasure in the very act of assembly—in the process, their instinct is satisfied to the same extent that the instinct of the born 'masters' (that is, the solitary predatory species of man) is deeply irritated and disturbed by organization. In every oligarchy—the whole of history teaches us this—the desire for *tyranny* always lies hidden; a continual tremor runs through every oligarchy as a result of the tension necessarily produced in each individual by the effort to control this desire. (So it was in *Greece*, for example: Plato attests to it in a hundred places, Plato, who knew his kind—*and* himself...)

19

The means of the ascetic priest which we have encountered so far—complete dampening of the feeling of life, mechanical activity, modest pleasures, foremost among these being love of one's neighbour, organization in herds, the awakening of a communal feeling of power, by means of which the individual's frustration with himself is submerged by his pleasure in the thriving of the community—these are all, according to modern criteria, *innocent* means in the struggle against listlessness: let us now turn to the more interesting means, the 'guilty' ones. These all involve one thing: some *excess of emotion*—used as the most effective means of anaesthetizing chronic pain and its numbing paralysis. This explains why priests have shown almost inexhaustible ingenuity in exploring the implications of this one question: '*How* is an excess of emotion to be attained?'... That sounds harsh: it would obviously sound nicer and perhaps less unpleasant to the ear if, for instance, I said: 'The ascetic priest has always exploited the *enthusiasm* which exists in all strong feelings.' But why continue to stroke the softened ears of our modern tender souls? Why should we *for our part* concede as much as a yard to their verbal hypocrisy? For us psychologists, that would represent an *act* of hypocrisy, not to mention the fact that it would turn our stomachs. For the *good taste* (—others might say: the honesty) of a psychologist today is manifested, if anywhere, in his resistance to the shamefully *moralized* form of speech which is smeared over practically all modern judgements of men and things. Make no mistake here: the most distinctive characteristic of modern souls and modern books is not lying, but an ingrained *innocence* in moral deception. To be obliged time and again to uncover this 'innocence' everywhere—that constitutes perhaps the most repulsive aspect of our work, of all the not-undangerous work which a psychologist has to undertake today; it represents a great danger *for us*—a danger which might lead even *us* to great disgust... I have no doubt as to the *only* use which modern books could serve (assuming that they last, which admittedly need not be feared, and also assuming that at some time there will exist a posterity whose taste will be stricter, more severe, *healthier*)—as to the use which everything modern would serve, could serve for this posterity: as an emetic—on account of its moral sweetness and falsity, its innermost feminism, which likes to go by the name of 'Idealism'* and in any case believes itself to be Idealism. Our intellectuals of today, our 'good men', do not tell lies—that much is true; but this does them *not the slightest* credit! The real lie, the genuine, resolute, 'honest' lie (on whose value Plato should be consulted) would be something far too severe, too strong for them; it would ask of them what *may not* be asked of them, that they should open their eyes to themselves, that they should know how to distinguish between 'true' and 'false' with respect to themselves. Only the *dishonest lie** is worthy of them; today, anyone who feels himself to be a 'good man' is completely incapable of taking any stance on any matter whatsoever other than one of *dishonest deceit*, deceit which is unfathomable, but innocent, faithful, blue-eyed, and virtuous. These 'good men'—they are all now thoroughly moralized, wrecked and ruined to all eternity as far as honesty is concerned: who among them could bear another *truth* about man!... Or, in more concrete terms: who among them could bear a *true* biography!... A few indications: Lord Byron kept a record of some very intimate personal matters, but Thomas Moore* was 'too good' for that: he burnt his friend's papers. Dr Gwinner,* the executor of Schopenhauer's will, supposedly did the same: for Schopenhauer too had made some written observations about himself and perhaps also against himself ('*eis heauton*'*). The diligent American Thayer,* Beethoven's biographer, suddenly stopped short in his work: having arrived at some point or other of this venerable and naïve life, he could stand it no longer... The moral of all this: which prudent man today would still write an honest word about himself?—to do so, he would have to be a member of the Order of Holy Foolhardiness. We are promised an autobiography by Richard Wagner: who doubts but that it will be a *prudent* autobiography?... Finally, let us recall the ludicrous indignation which the Catholic priest Janssen* aroused in Germany with his inconceivably straightforward and harmless picture of the German Reformation movement; what would happen if for once someone were to tell the story of this movement *differently*, if for once a real psychologist were to tell the story of a real Luther, not with the moral simplicity of a country priest, not with the sickly-sweet and respectful discretion of Protestant historians, but with the fearlessness of a Taine,* for instance, from inner *strength of soul* rather than from prudent respect for strength?... (The Germans, incidentally, have recently produced a beautiful enough example of the classical type of the latter—they would be entitled to claim him for themselves, and to pride themselves upon having produced him: Leopold Ranke*, the born classical *advocatus** of every *causa fortior*,* the most prudent of all prudent 'realists'.)

20

But my point will have been taken—there is reason enough, all in all, for our inability, as psychologists of today, to shake off a degree of mistrust *towards ourselves*... We too are probably still too good for our work, still the victims, the prey, the sick men of this moralized taste of the time, however much we feel ourselves to be those who despise it—it probably infects even *us*. What was the warning that diplomat* gave when he addressed his colleagues? 'Let us be wary above all of our first impulses!' he said, '*they are almost always good*'... This is the way in which every psychologist today should address his colleagues... And here we return to our problem, which does indeed require some severity, some mistrust on our part, in particular towards 'first impulses'. *The ascetic ideal employed to stimulate an excess of emotion*—anyone who remembers the preceding essay will already anticipate the essence of what remains to be presented, compressed as it is into these ten words. To tear the human soul loose from its moorings, to immerse it in fear, frost, intense heat, and delight to the point that it breaks free like a bolt of lightning from all the narrowness and pettiness of listlessness, of dullness, of disgruntlement: which paths lead to *this* goal? And which are the most reliable?... Fundamentally, every great feeling has this capacity, provided that it is discharged suddenly—wrath, fear, lust, revenge, hope, triumph, despair, cruelty; and the ascetic priest has indeed harnessed for his own designs this *entire* pack of wild dogs, sometimes unleashing this one, sometimes that one, and always to the same end, that is, in order to rouse man from his lethargic sadness, to put to flight, even if only for a time, his dull pain, his miserable hesitation, and always under cover of a religious interpretation and 'justification'. Each of these excesses of emotion has to be *paid for* afterwards, as goes without saying—each makes the sick man sicker—: and so this kind of remedy for pain is, according to modern criteria, a 'guilty' kind. Yet one must, to be fair, insist all the more upon the fact that it is applied in *good conscience*, that the ascetic priest prescribed it in the most profound belief in its usefulness, even its indispensability—and often enough he almost broke himself through the misery which he created. Furthermore, one must insist upon the fact that vehement physiological reactions to such excesses, perhaps even taking the form of mental disturbances, do not ultimately refute the sense of this kind of medication: which, as has been demonstrated earlier, aims not to heal sickness but to combat the listlessness of depression, to alleviate and anaesthetize it. And this goal was indeed attained *by these means*. The master-stroke which the ascetic priest permitted himself in order to play heart-rending and enraptured music of all kinds upon the human soul was—as everyone knows—his exploitation of the *sense of guilt*. The preceding essay alluded briefly to the origin of this sense of guilt—as a piece of animal psychology, nothing more: there we encountered the feeling of guilt in its raw state, so to speak. Only in the hands of the priest, this real artist in guilty feelings, did it take form—oh what a form! 'Sin', for such is the priestly name given to the reinterpretation of animal 'bad conscience' (cruelty turned inwards against itself)—has been the greatest event so far in the history of the sick soul: it represents the most dangerous and fateful trick of religious interpretation. Man, suffering from himself in some way, suffering physiologically in any case, like an animal locked in a cage, uncertain as to why and wherefore, desiring reasons—reasons are a relief—desiring means and narcotics, finally consults someone who is also acquainted with hidden things—and behold! he receives a hint, he receives from a magician, from the ascetic priest, the first hint as to the 'cause' of his suffering: he is to seek it in *himself*, in some *guilt*, in a piece of the past, he should understand his suffering itself as a *state of punishment*... He has heard, he has understood, the unfortunate man: now he is in a situation like that of the hen around which a line is drawn. Never again does he escape this circle of lines: out of the sick man a 'sinner' is made... For two millennia now, it has been impossible to escape the sight of this new sick man, the 'sinner'—will this ever change? No matter where one looks, one meets the hypnotic gaze of the sinner, always moving in the same direction (in the direction of 'guilt', as the *sole* cause of suffering); everywhere the evil conscience, this '*abominable beast*', to use Luther's phrase; everywhere the regurgitation of the past, the distortion of the deed, the 'jaundiced eye' for all activity; everywhere the *will* to misunderstand suffering, its reinterpretation into feelings of guilt, the content of life reduced to fear and punishment; everywhere the whip, the hair-shirt, the starving body, remorse; everywhere the sinner stretching himself on the cruel rack of a restless, sickly, lascivious conscience;

everywhere the dumb pain, the most extreme fear, the agony of the tortured heart, the cramps of an unknown happiness, the cry for 'redemption'. And by means of this system of procedures the old depression, lethargy, and fatigue was indeed thoroughly *overcome*, life became *very* interesting once again: awake, eternally awake, sleepless, glowing, charred, exhausted and yet not tired—this was what distinguished the man, the 'sinner' who had been initiated into *these* mysteries. This great old magician struggling against listlessness, the ascetic priest—he had obviously succeeded, *his* kingdom had come: no longer did one lament pain, one *craved* pain; '*more* pain! *more* pain!', his disciples and initiates have for centuries cried yearningly. Every painful excess of emotion, everything which shattered, overturned, crushed, transported, enraptured, the secret of the torture-chambers, the ingenuity of hell itself—all this from now on lay uncovered, surmised, exploited, all this stood at the disposal of the magician, all this served the end of the victory of his ideal, the ascetic ideal... 'My kingdom is not of *this* world'*—he said as before; was he really entitled to say this?... Goethe asserted that there were only thirty-six tragic situations:* from this one could guess, if one did not already know, that Goethe was no ascetic priest. For the ascetic priest—*he* knows more...

21

To indulge in criticism of *this* kind of priestly medication, the 'guilty' kind, in its entirety is an idle pastime. Who would wish to maintain that such an excess of emotion as the ascetic priest usually prescribes to his sick men (under the holiest name, as goes without saying, and likewise thoroughly steeped in the holiness of his goal), was ever of actual *benefit* to any of them? We should agree at least as to what is meant by 'benefit'. If one wishes to suggest that such a system of treatment has *improved* man, I will not dispute that: I would only add what I understand by 'improved'—much the same as 'tamed', 'weakened', 'discouraged', 'refined', 'pampered', 'emasculated' (much the same, then, as *damaged*...). But when it is administered to the sick, the disgruntled, and the depressed, then such a system always makes the sick man *sicker*, even if it makes him 'better'; one should ask the psychiatrists what happens when the torture of repentance, remorse, and cramps of redemption are methodically administered. One should consult history too; wherever the ascetic priest has implemented this treatment of the sick, sickness has always spread and deepened with sinister speed. What has been the constant sign of its 'success'? A ruined nervous system in addition to what was otherwise already sick; and that on the largest and on the smallest scale, for the individual as for the masses. In the wake of training* for repentance and redemption we find huge epidemics of epilepsy, the greatest known to history, like that of the St Vitus's and St John's dancers* of the Middle Ages; we find another of its consequences in terrible paralysis and prolonged depressions, which can definitively reverse the temperament of a people or of a town (Geneva, Basle);—here we might also include the hysteria of the witch-hunt, something related to somnambulism (there were eight great epidemic outbreaks of this between 1564 and 1605 alone)—; likewise we find in its wake that mass delirium of the death-wish whose horrific cry, '*evviva la morte!*',* was heard throughout Europe and beyond, interrupted sometimes by lascivious idiosyncrasies, sometimes by destructive fury: just as the same mutability of feeling, with the same intermittences and interruptions, can be seen even today wherever the ascetic doctrine of sin attains another great success. (The religious neurosis* *appears* as a form of 'evil': there is no doubt about that. But what is it? *Quaeritur.**) Broadly speaking, the ascetic ideal and its cult of sublime morality, this most ingenious, most unscrupulous, and most dangerous systematization of all the means towards excess of emotion concealed beneath the cloak of holy intentions, has thus carved its fearful and unforgettable inscription into the whole history of mankind; and, unfortunately, into *more* than just its history... I would be hard pressed to find anything else which has insinuated itself into the *health* and strength of a race—of the Europeans, that is—to the same destructive extent as this ideal; one might without any exaggeration call this *the true disaster* in the history of the health of European man. The only thing which even comes close in terms of destructive effect is the specifically Germanic influence: by that, I mean the poisoning of Europe with alcohol, which has up to now kept strict pace with the political and racial predominance of the Germans (—wherever they infused their blood, they also infused their vice).—Syphilis might be mentioned as third in line—*magno sed proxima intervallo*.*

22

Wherever he has come to dominance, the ascetic priest has ruined the health of the mind; as a consequence, he has also ruined *taste in artibus et litteris**—and he continues to do so. 'As a consequence?'—I hope that one will simply grant me this 'as a consequence'; I at least have no wish to set about proving it. Just a single hint: it concerns the fundamental book of Christian literature, its real model, its 'book in itself'. Even in the midst of Greco-Roman splendour, which was also an age of literary splendour, in the face of an ancient world of writing not yet withered and smashed, at a time when it was still possible to read books for which one would nowadays exchange half of some literatures, the simplicity and vanity of Christian agitators—they are called Church Fathers—had the temerity to decree: '*We* too have our classical literature, *we do not need that of the Greeks*'—and with that they pointed proudly to books of legend, the letters of the Apostles, little tracts and apologias, in much the same way as the 'Salvation Army'* in England today conducts its campaign against Shakespeare and other 'heathens' with a similar literature. I have no love for the 'New Testament', you will already have guessed; it almost disturbs me to find myself so isolated in a matter of taste as regards this most appeciated, over-appreciated written work (the taste of two thousand years is *against* me): but there it is! 'Here I stand, I can do no other'*—I have the courage of my bad taste. The *Old* Testament—now that is a completely different matter: all honour to the Old Testament! There I find great men, a heroic landscape, and something of that rarest quality on earth, the incomparable naïveté of the *strong heart*; what is more, I find a people. But in the New Testament, on the other hand, I find only the petty business of sects, mere rococo* of the soul, mere embellishment, nooks and crannies, strange things, the air of the meeting-house, not forgetting an occasional breath of bucolic sentimentality which belongs to the period (*and* to the Roman province), and is not so much Jewish as Hellenistic. Humility and self-importance side by side; a garrulousness of feeling, which verges on the stupefying; passionate enthusiasm rather than passion itself; an embarrassing game of gestures; there is no visible trace of any good upbringing. How can one make so much of one's petty weaknesses as these pious little men do! No one asks it of them; certainly not God. Ultimately, all these petty people from the provinces want 'the crown of eternal life';* but to what end? what for?—one could not be more presumptuous. An 'immortal' Peter: who could bear *him*! Their ambition is laughable: *they* regurgitate what is most personal, their stupidities, sadnesses, and the worries of the idle loafer, as if the in-itself of things is obliged to concern itself with them; *they* never tire of implicating God in the pettiest misery which involves them. And this perpetual familiarity of the worst taste with God! This Jewish, and not merely Jewish, worrying and pawing intrusiveness towards God!... There are despised little 'heathen peoples' in East Asia who could have taught these first Christians something essential, some *tact* in veneration; as Christian missionaries attest, they do not so much as permit themselves to utter the name of their god. This seems delicate enough to me; it is certainly too delicate for the 'first' Christians, and not only the first: in order to appreciate the contrast, remember Luther, for instance, the 'most eloquent' and most presumptuous peasant whom Germany has produced, and the tone he preferred to adopt when talking with God. Luther's resistance to the mediating saints of the Church (in particular, to '*the Devil's sow, the Pope*') was, there is no doubt, at bottom the resistance of a lout frustrated by the *good etiquette* of the Church, the reverential etiquette of hieratic taste which admits only the more initiated and more silent into the holy of holies and bars it to the louts. Here of all places these louts were to be refused a say once and for all—but Luther, the peasant, wanted things to be completely different, they did not seem sufficiently *German* to him in this form: he wanted above all to talk directly to his God, to talk to Him for himself, to talk to Him 'without airs and graces'... Well, this he did.—The ascetic ideal, as one may surmise, has never been a school of good taste, even less of good manners—it was at best a school of hieratic manners—: this is because its composition includes something which is a mortal enemy of all good manners—lack of moderation, aversion to moderation, it is itself a '*non plus ultra*'.*

23

The ascetic ideal has ruined not only health and taste, but also a third, fourth, fifth, sixth thing—I will refrain from listing *all* the things it has ruined (when would I come to the end!). It is not my intention here to bring to light the effects of this ideal but rather only what it *means*, what it implies, what lies hidden behind it, under it, in it, what it expresses in a provisional and obscure way, overlaid with question-marks and misunderstandings. And only with respect to *this* goal was I entitled to subject my readers to the sight of its monstrous and disastrous effects: by way of preparation, that is, for the ultimate and most terrifying sight which the investigation of the meaning of this ideal holds for me. For what is the meaning of the power of this ideal, what is the meaning of the *monstrous nature* of its power? Why has it been granted this amount of space? Why has it not met with more effective resistance? The ascetic ideal expresses a will: *where* is the opposing will which expresses an *opposing ideal*? The ascetic ideal has a *goal*—and this goal is sufficiently universal for all other interests of human existence to seem narrow and petty in comparison; it relentlessly interprets periods, peoples, men in terms of this goal, it allows no other interpretation, no other goal, it reproaches, negates, affirms, confirms exclusively with reference to *its* interpretation (—and has there ever existed a system of interpretation more fully thought through to its end?); it subordinates itself to no other power, it believes rather in its prerogative over all other powers, in its absolute *seniority of rank* with respect to all other powers—it believes that no power can exist on earth without first having had conferred upon it a meaning, a right to existence, a value as an instrument in the service of *its* work, as a path and means to *its* goal, to its *single* goal... Where is the opposition to this closed system of will, goal, and interpretation? Why does no opposition *exist*? Where is the *other* '*single* goal'? But I am told that such opposition does *exist*, that it has not only fought a long and successful campaign against that ideal but has even already overcome it in all important respects: the whole of our modern *science** supposedly bears witness to this fact—this modern science, which, as a genuine philosophy of reality, clearly believes only in itself, clearly possesses the courage to be itself, the will to itself, and has managed well enough up to now without God, the beyond, and the virtues of denial. However, such noisy agitators' chatter has no effect on me: these trumpeters of reality are bad musicians, it is clear from the sound they make that their voices do *not* rise up from the depths, that the abyss of the scientific conscience—for today the scientific conscience is an abyss—does *not* speak through them, that the word 'science' in the mouths of such trumpeters is simply an obscenity, an abuse, an example of impudence. The very opposite of what is being asserted here is the truth: science today has simply *no* belief in itself, let alone an ideal *above* it—and where it survives at all as passion, love, glowing intensity, *suffering*, it constitutes not the opposite of the ascetic ideal but rather *its most recent and most refined form*. Does that sound alienating to you?... For there are enough good and modest working folk even among today's scholars, who are content in their little corner and, because they are content there, sometimes a little presumptuously voice the demand that in general one *should* be content with things today, particularly in science, where so many useful things remain to be done. I do not dispute this; the last thing I would want to do is to spoil the enjoyment which these honest workers take in their craft: for their work gives me pleasure. But the fact that there is disciplined work being done in science and that there are contented workers *fails* to prove that today science as a whole has a goal, a will, an ideal, a passion of great conviction. The opposite, as I said, is the case: where it is not the most recent manifestation of the ascetic ideal—the instances involved here are too few, refined, and exceptional to refute the general case—science today is a *hiding-place* for all kinds of discontent, lack of conviction, gnawing worm, *despectio sui*,* bad conscience—it is none other than the *restlessness* which results from lack of ideals, a form of suffering from a *lack* of any great love, from dissatisfaction with an *involuntary* temperance. Oh what does science not conceal today! how much, at least, it is *supposed* to conceal! The diligence of our best scholars, their heedless industry, the smoke rising from their heads by day and night, their mastery of the craft itself—how often the real meaning of all this consists in keeping something hidden from oneself! Science as a means of self-anaesthesis: *are you familiar with that?*... Anyone who keeps the company of scholars has had on occasion the experience of wounding them to the quick with a harmless word, one embitters and alienates one's scholar friends at the very moment of intending to honour them, one throws them into a wild rage simply because one is too insensitive to realize with whom one is actually dealing, with men who *suffer* but refuse to admit as much to themselves, with anaesthetized and insensate men who fear one thing only: *being brought to consciousness*...

24

—And now take a look at those rarer cases of which I spoke, the last surviving idealists among philosophers and scholars today: are they perhaps the sought-for *opponents* of the ascetic ideal, its *counter-idealists*? This, in fact, is what they *believe* themselves to be, these 'unbelievers' (for this is what they all are); opposition to this ideal seems to be their very last article of faith, they are so earnest on this point, so passionate their words, their gestures then become—but does this necessarily make what they believe *true*?... We 'seekers after knowledge' are suspicious of virtually every kind of believer; our mistrust has gradually taught us to infer the opposite of what was previously inferred: wherever the strength of a belief comes clearly to the fore, we assume a certain weakness in the proof, even a certain *improbability* in what is believed. It is not that we deny that belief 'makes one blessed': *this is the very reason* why we deny that belief *proves* anything—a strong belief which 'makes one blessed' arouses suspicion of what is believed, it does not establish 'truth', it establishes a certain probability—of *illusion*. How do things stand in the present case?—These deniers and outsiders of today, these absolutists in a single respect—in their claim to intellectual hygiene—these hard, severe, abstemious, heroic spirits, who constitute the pride of our age, all these pale atheists, anti-Christians, immoralists, nihilists, these spiritual sceptics, ephectics,* *hectic* ones (for this is what they all are in some sense or other); these last idealists of knowledge, these men in whom the intellectual conscience is alone embodied and dwells today—they believe themselves to be as free as possible from the ascetic ideal, these 'free, *very* free spirits': and yet, if I may reveal to them what they themselves cannot see—for they are too close to themselves—: this self-same ideal is *their* ideal too, they themselves are perhaps its sole representatives today, they themselves are its most spiritualized product, its most advanced party of warriors and scouts, its most insidious, most delicate, least tangible form of seduction—if I am in anything a solver of enigmas, then let me be so now with *this* proposition!... These men are far from *free* spirits: *for they still believe in the truth!*... When the Christian crusaders in the Orient came upon that invincible order of the Assassins,* that order of free spirits *par excellence*, whose lowest grade lived in an obedience which no order of monks has attained, they somehow received a hint of that symbol and watchword which was reserved for only the highest grades as their *secretum*:* 'Nothing is true, everything is permitted'... Well now, *that* was *freedom* of spirit indeed, *thus* even the belief in truth was *dismissed*... Has any European, any Christian free spirit ever strayed within this proposition and its labyrinthine *consequences*? does he know the Minotaur* of this cave *from experience*?... I doubt it; more, I know that it is not so—nothing is more foreign to these men who are absolutists in a *single* respect, these *so-called* 'free spirits', than freedom and liberation in that sense; indeed, in no respect are they more tightly bound; it is in their very belief in truth that they are more inflexible and absolute than anyone else. Perhaps I am too familiar with all of this: the venerable abstemiousness which such a belief requires of philosophers, the stoicism of the intellect which renounces negation with the same severity as affirmation, the desire to stop short at the factual, the *factum brutum*, that fatalism of '*petits faits*' (*ce petit faitalisme*,* as I call it), in which French science is now seeking a kind of moral superiority over German science, the complete renunciation of interpretation (of violating, adapting, abridging, omitting, padding out, spinning out, re-falsifying, and whatever else belongs to the *essence* of all interpretation)—all this expresses, broadly speaking, the asceticism of virtue as much as it expresses some kind of denial of sensuality (it is basically only a particular mode of this denial). But what *compels* these men to this absolute will to truth, albeit as its unconscious imperative, is the *belief in the ascetic ideal itself*—make no mistake on this point—it is the belief in a *metaphysical* value, the value of *truth in itself*, as it alone is guaranteed and attested in each ideal (it stands or falls with each ideal). Strictly speaking, there is absolutely no science 'without presuppositions', the very idea is inconceivable, paralogical: a philosophy, a 'belief' must always exist first in order for science to derive from it a direction, a meaning, a limit, a method, a *right* to existence. (Anyone who understands things the other way round, who is prepared, for example, to establish philosophy 'on a strictly scientific basis', must first turn not only philosophy but also truth itself *on their heads*: the worst possible insult to decency with respect to two such venerable ladies!) Yes, there is no doubt—and here I will let my *Gay Science* have its say—compare Book Five, §334:—'the truthful man, in the bold and ultimate sense presupposed by the belief in science, *affirms in the process another world* from that of life, nature, and history; and in so far as he affirms this "other world", what? must he not then in the process—deny its counterpart, this world, *our* world?... The belief upon which our science rests remains a *metaphysical belief*. We seekers after knowledge today, we godless ones and anti-metaphysicians, we too continue to take *our* flame from that fire ignited by a belief which is millennia old, that Christian belief, which was also Plato's belief, that God is the truth, that the truth is *divine*... But what if this self-same idea is becoming increasingly incredible, what if nothing any longer reveals itself as divine, apart from error, blindness, lies—what if God himself proves to be our *oldest lie*?'— —At this point, one must pause for a long period of reflection. From this moment on, science itself *requires* justification (which is not to say that such justification exists). On this question, consider the oldest and the most recent philosophies: they all lack an awareness of the extent to which the will to truth itself first requires justification, there is a gap in every philosophy at this point—why is that? Because up to now the ascetic ideal has *dominated* all philosophy, because truth was posited as being, as God, as the highest instance itself, because it was *not permitted* that truth should be a problem. Is this 'permitted' understood?—From the moment when belief in the God of the ascetic ideal is denied, *a new problem exists*: that of the *value* of truth.—The will to truth requires critique—let us define our own task in this way—the value of truth must for once, by way of experiment, be *called into question*... (Anyone who finds this overly terse is referred to the section of *The Gay Science* entitled: 'To What Extent We Remain Pious', and better, to the whole of Book Five of that work, as well as the Preface to *Daybreak*.)

25

No! Do not come to me with science when I am looking for the natural antagonist of the ascetic ideal, when I ask: 'Where is the opposing will, which expresses its *opposing ideal*?' It is a long time since science has been independent enough for that, it first requires a value-ideal, a value-creating power, in whose service it is *allowed to believe* in itself—it never creates values itself. Its relationship to the ascetic ideal is in itself by no means antagonistic; rather, for the most part, it provides the impetus for the latter's inner development. On closer scrutiny, its contradiction and struggle does not refer at all to the ascetic ideal itself, but only to its outworks, its disguise, its play of masks, to its occasional tendency to become rigid, wooden, and dogmatic—science sets the life within it free once again by denying what is exoteric to it. These two, science and the ascetic ideal, share the same foundation—I have already indicated as much—: that is, the same overestimation of the truth (more accurately: the same belief that the truth is *above* evaluation and criticism). They are, then, *necessarily* allies—so that, if they are to be resisted, they must be resisted and called into question together. A depreciation of the ascetic ideal inevitably entails a depreciation of science: keep your eyes and ears open for occasional indications of this! (*Art*, let me say in advance, for I will at some stage return to this idea at greater length—art, in which the *lie* is sanctified and the *will to deceive* has good conscience on its side, is much more fundamentally opposed to the ascetic ideal than science: Plato, the greatest enemy of art which Europe has so far produced, felt this instinctively. Plato versus Homer: that is the complete, the real antagonism—on one side, the sincerest 'man of the beyond', the philosopher who most defames life; on the other, the poet who involuntarily deifies it, the *golden* nature. The artist in the service of the ascetic ideal is therefore the most essential *corruption* of the artist possible, and unfortunately one of the most common: for nothing is more venal than an artist.) Even when examined from the point of view of physiology, science rests on the same foundation as the ascetic ideal: both presuppose a certain *impoverishment of life*—a cooling of the feelings, a slowing of the tempo, dialectic in place of instinct, the impression of *seriousness* upon face and gesture (seriousness, the most unmistakable sign of a straining metabolism, of an increasingly arduous struggle for life). Take a look at the periods in the history of a people in which the scholar comes to the fore: they are times of exhaustion, often of twilight, of decline—the overflowing strength, the certainty of life, the certainty of the *future* are things of the past. The predominance of mandarins is never a good sign: just as little as the advent of democracy, of international courts of peace instead of wars, of equal rights for women, of the religion of compassion, and whatever other symptoms there are of life in decline. (Science itself understood as a problem; what is the meaning of science?—compare on this subject the Preface to *The Birth of Tragedy*.)—No! this 'modern science'—only open your eyes to it!—is at present the *best* ally of the ascetic ideal, precisely because it is the least conscious, the most involuntary, the most sinister, and the most subterranean! Up to now they have played the *same* game, the 'poor in spirit'* and the opponents of this ideal (incidentally, beware of thinking that these latter represent the opposite of the former, the *rich* in spirit, for instance—*that* they are most definitely *not*, I named them hectic ones of the spirit). As for the latter's famous *victories*: they are undoubtedly victories—but over what? They certainly do not represent the defeat of the ascetic ideal, which has rather been strengthened, rendered less tangible, more spiritual, more insidious by the fact that science has once again mercilessly broken down a wall, an outwork which had been built on to it and had *coarsened* its appearance. Does anyone really think, for instance, that the defeat of theological astronomy* represented a defeat for the ideal?... Is man perhaps *less in need* of a transcendental solution to his enigmatic existence now that this existence seems more conspicuously random, idle, and dispensable within the *visible* order of things? Is the very self-belittlement of man, his *will* to self-belittlement since Copernicus,* not continuing its inexorable progress? Oh, the belief in his worth, uniqueness, irreplaceability in the chain of being is a thing of the past—he has become an animal, an animal in the literal sense, without qualification or reservation, he, who previously believed himself almost a god ('child of God', 'demigod')... Since Copernicus, man seems to have been on a steep slope—from now on he rolls faster and faster away from the centre—in what direction? towards nothingness? towards the '*piercing* feeling of his nothingness'?... Well now! and is this not the very path which leads directly back—to the *old* ideal?... *All* science (and not only astronomy, on the subject of whose humiliating and humbling effect Kant made a remarkable admission, 'it annihilates my importance'*), all science, natural as well as *unnatural*—my name for the self-criticism of knowledge—today aims to talk man out of his previous self-respect, as if it had been nothing more than a conceited delusion. One might even say that today its own pride, its own bitter form of Stoic ataraxie,* rests in maintaining man's laboriously achieved *self-contempt* as his last, most serious claim to self-respect (and rightly so, in fact: for someone who feels contempt has still not 'forgotten how to respect'...). Does this really represent *active opposition* to the ascetic ideal? Does one really in all seriousness still think (as the theologians deluded themselves for a while) that, for instance, Kant's victory over the conceptual dogma of theology* ('God', 'soul', 'freedom', 'immortality') harmed that ideal?—and in this matter it should not even concern us whether Kant ever intended anything of the sort. What is certain is that, since Kant, all kinds of transcendentalists have once again won the day—they are liberated from the theologians: what luck!—Kant revealed to them the secret path along which they may from now on, in independence and with the greatest scientific respectability, pursue their 'heart's desire'. Likewise: from now on, who could hold it against the agnostics if, as worshippers of the unknown and mysterious in itself, they now pray to the *question-mark itself* as God? (Xaver Doudan* talks at one point about the *ravages* caused by '*l'habitude d'admirer l'inintelligible au lieu de rester tout simplement dans l'inconnu*';* he imagined that the ancients had avoided this.) Assuming that everything which man 'knows' fails to satisfy his desires but rather frustrates them and engenders fear, what a divine liberation it is to be allowed to attribute the blame for this not to 'desire' but to 'knowledge'!... 'There is no knowledge: *consequently*—there is a God': what a new *elegantia syllogismi*!* what a *triumph* of the ascetic ideal!—

26

—Or perhaps modern historiography as a whole displays an attitude which is more certain of life, more certain of the ideal? Its most refined aspiration now is to the status of *mirror*; it rejects all teleology; it no longer has the slightest desire to 'prove' anything; it disdains the opportunity of playing the judge and deems this a matter of good taste—it affirms as little as it denies, it ascertains, it 'describes'... All this is ascetic to a high degree; but it is at the same time and to an even higher degree *nihilistic*, make no mistake! One sees a sad, hard, but determined gaze—an eye which *looks out*, as an isolated Arctic explorer looks out (perhaps in order not to look in? in order not to look back?...). Here is snow, here life is silenced; the last crows whose cries can still be heard here are called 'Why?', 'In vain!', '*Nada*!'*—nothing grows and thrives here any longer, at most the metapolitics of St Petersburg* and Tolstoyan 'compassion'.* As for that other kind of historian, an even more modern kind, perhaps, hedonistic and lascivious, who flirts with life as much as with the ascetic ideal, who uses the word 'artist' as a glove and has today completely monopolized the praise of contemplation: oh how these sweet wits make one yearn even for ascetics and winter landscapes! No! the Devil take these 'contemplative' people! I would much prefer wandering through the gloomiest, grey, freezing fog with the historical nihilists!—It should not come to that, even if I had to choose to listen to a completely unhistorical, anti-historical man (such as Dühring, whose voice is today in Germany intoxicating what has so far remained a timid and still-unavowed species of 'beautiful soul', the *species anarchista** within the educated proletariat). The 'contemplative men' are a hundred times worse—: nothing so disgusts me as this kind of 'objective' armchair scholar, a scented little historical hedonist, half-Pope, half-satyr, with his perfume by Renan* and his high falsetto applause immediately revealing what he is lacking and *where*, *where* the Fates* have in this case applied their cruel shears in an oh! all too surgical manner! This offends my taste, and also tries my patience: let him who has nothing to lose by it remain a patient onlooker—such a sight makes me furious, such 'spectators' make me feel embittered towards the 'theatre', more so than towards theatre in general (the theatre of history, you understand), I am subject to sudden Anacreontic* moods: Nature which gave the bull its horns and the lion its *chasm'odonton* why did Nature give me my foot?... For kicking, by holy Anacreon! and not just for running away; for kicking in these crumbling armchairs, this cowardly contemplation, this prurient impotence in the face of history, this flirtation with ascetic ideals, this Tartufferie* which is the justice of the emasculated! I have the greatest respect for the ascetic ideal, *in so far as it is honest!* as long as it believes in itself and refrains from farcical play-acting! But I dislike all these coquettish little bugs—whose insatiable ambition is to give off the smell of the infinite, until ultimately the infinite smells of bugs; I dislike redecorated graves which play the part of life; I dislike the tired and used-up men who wrap themselves in wisdom and have an 'objective' view; I dislike agitators who dress up as heroes and disguise their old broom of a head under a magic cap of ideals; I dislike ambitious artists who aspire to represent the ascetic and the priest and who are at bottom no more than tragic clowns; nor do I like these most recent speculators in idealism, the anti-Semites, who, rolling their eyes in a Christian-Aryan-Philistine way, seek to rouse all the bovine elements of the people through an exasperating abuse of the cheapest means of agitation and moral attitudes (—that every kind of intellectual swindle achieves some degree of success in the Germany of today is linked to the virtually undeniable and already tangible *stultification* of the German mind, whose cause I seek in an all-too exclusive diet of newspapers, politics, beer, and Wagnerian music, including what this diet presupposes: first of all the constriction and vanity characteristic of the nation, the strong but narrow principle of 'Deutschland, Deutschland über alles',* as well as the *paralysis agitans** of 'modern ideas'). Europe today is above all rich and inventive in means of stimulation, its greatest need seems to be for stimulants and strong spirits; hence also the monstrous amount of forgery in ideals, that most powerful alcohol of the spirit, hence also the repulsive, foul-smelling, deceitful, pseudo-alcoholic atmosphere everywhere. I should like to know how many shiploads of imitated idealism, of heroic costumes and big words which rattle like tin, how many tons of sugary spirits of compassion (producer: *la religion de la souffrance**), how many wooden-legs of 'righteous indignation' for the aid of the spiritually flat-footed, how many *play-actors* of the Christian-moral ideal one would have to export from Europe today before the air began to smell pure once again... Obviously, this over-production represents a new opportunity for *trade*, obviously a new 'business' could be made out of these little ideal-idols and the accompanying 'idealists'—do not miss the hint! Who is brave enough to take it up?—we hold in our *hands* the opportunity of *idealizing* the whole world!... But what am I saying about bravery: only one thing is required here—the right hands for the job, uninhibited, very uninhibited hands...

27

—Enough! Enough! Let us leave behind these curiosities and complexities of the most modern spirit which give us as much cause for laughter as frustration: since *our* problem, the problem of the *meaning* of the ascetic ideal may dispense with them—what does this problem have to do with yesterday and today! I shall deal with these things more thoroughly and severely in another connection (under the title 'On the History of European Nihilism'; for this I refer the reader to my work in progress: *The Will to Power: An Attempt at a Transvaluation of all Values**). My exclusive concern here has been to indicate that, even in the spiritual sphere, there is still only one kind of enemy who is capable of causing the ascetic ideal real *harm*: those play-actors who act out this ideal—for they arouse suspicion. Otherwise, wherever the spirit is at work today, severe, powerful, and without forgery, it dispenses completely with this ideal—the popular term for this abstinence is 'atheism'—*except for its will to truth*. But this will, this *remnant* of the ideal, is, if one is willing to believe me, the strictest, most spiritual formulation of the ideal itself, absolutely esoteric, stripped of all outworks—not so much its remnant, then, as its *core*. Absolute, honest atheism (—and *this* is the only air which we more spiritual men of this age breathe!) is *not* the antithesis of the ideal which it appears to be; it is rather only one of the last phases of its development, one of its ultimate forms and inner consequences—it is an awe-inspiring *catastrophe*, the outcome of a two-thousand-year training in truthfulness, which finally forbids itself the *lie of belief in God*. (That the same development occurs completely independently in India should prove something: the same ideal compelling the same conclusion; the decisive point having already been reached five centuries before the European calendar, with Buddha, or more accurately: with the Sankhya philosophy,* which was then popularized and turned into a religion by Buddha.) What, strictly speaking, really *defeated* the Christian God? The answer can be found in my *Gay Science* (§357): 'Christian morality itself, the increasing seriousness with which the concept of truthfulness was taken, the refinement of the Christian conscience in confession, translated and sublimated into the scientific conscience, into intellectual hygiene at all costs. To view nature as if it were proof of the goodness and protection of a God; to interpret history to the honour of a divine reason, as continual witness to a moral world-order and its ultimate moral intentions; to explain one's own experiences, as pious people have for long enough explained them, as if everything were predetermined, everything a sign, everything designed to promote the redemption of the soul: that time is *past*, it has conscience *against* it, it seems to all finer consciences indecent, dishonest, deceitful, feminism, weakness, cowardice—in this rigour, if in anything, we are *good Europeans* and heirs to Europe's longest and boldest process of self-overcoming.' All great things are the cause of their own destruction, through an act of self-cancellation: the law of life, the law of *necessary* 'self-overcoming'* which is the essence of life, wills it so—ultimately, the call goes out to the legislator himself: '*patere legem, quam ipse tulisti*'.* In this way, Christianity *as dogma* was destroyed by its own morality; in this way, Christianity *as morality* must now be destroyed—we are standing on the threshold of *this* very event. After Christian truthfulness has drawn one conclusion after another, it finally draws its *strongest conclusion*, its conclusion *against* itself; this will occur when it asks the question: '*What is the meaning of all will to truth?*'... And here again I touch on my problem, on our problem, my *unknown* friends (—for as yet I *know* of no friend): what meaning would *our* whole being possess, if we were not those in whom this will to truth becomes conscious of itself as a *problem*?... There is no doubt that from now on morality will be *destroyed* through the coming to consciousness of the will to truth: this is the great drama in a hundred acts which is reserved for Europe over the next two thousand years, the most fearful, most questionable and perhaps also most hopeful of all dramas...

28

If we put aside the ascetic ideal, then man, the *animal* man, has had no meaning up to now. His existence on earth has lacked a goal: 'why does man exist at all?'—was a question without an answer; the *will* for man and earth was missing; behind every great human destiny rang the even greater refrain: 'In vain!' For the meaning of the ascetic ideal is none other than *this*: that something was missing, that man was surrounded by a gaping *void*—he did not know how to justify, explain, affirm himself, he *suffered* from the problem of his meaning. He suffered in other ways too, he was for the most part a *sickly* animal: his problem, however, was *not* suffering itself, but rather the absence of an answer to his questioning cry: '*Why* do I suffer?' Man, the boldest animal and the one most accustomed to pain, does *not* repudiate suffering as such; he *desires* it, he even seeks it out, provided that he has been shown a *meaning* for it, a *reason* for suffering. The meaninglessness of suffering, and *not* suffering as such, has been the curse which has hung over mankind up to now—*and the ascetic ideal offered mankind a meaning!* As yet, it has been the only meaning; and any meaning is better than no meaning; in every respect, the ascetic ideal has been the best '*faute de mieux*'* so far. It *explained* suffering; it seemed to fill the gaping void; the door was closed against all suicidal nihilism. The explanation—there is no doubt—brought new suffering with it, deeper, more internal, more poisonous, gnawing suffering: it brought all suffering under the perspective of *guilt*... But in spite of all this—or thanks to it—man was *saved*, he had a meaning, from now on he was no longer like a leaf in the wind, a plaything of absurdity, of the absence of meaning, from now on he was able to *will* something—it did not matter at first to what end, why, and with what means he exercised his will: *the will itself was saved*. We can no longer conceal from ourselves *what* this willing directed by the ascetic ideal actually expresses in its entirety: this hatred of the human, and even more of the animal, of the material, this revulsion from the senses, from reason itself, this fear of happiness and beauty, this yearning to pass beyond all appearance, change, becoming, death, desire, beyond yearning itself. All this represents—may we be bold enough to grasp this—a *will to nothingness*, an aversion to life, a rebellion against the most fundamental pre-conditions of life, but which is and remains none the less a *will*!... And, to say once again in conclusion what I said at the beginning: man would rather will *nothingness* than *not* will at all...

EXPLANATORY NOTES

3 *We remain unknown to ourselves*: allusion to the inscription above the cave of the oracle at Delphi—'Know thyself.'

We have never sought after ourselves: re-working of Matthew 7: 7—'Ask, and it shall be given you; seek and ye shall find; knock, and it shall be opened unto you.'

'Where your treasure is, there will your heart be also': Matthew 6: 21.

'Everyone is furthest from himself': re-working of Terence, *Andria* (*The Girl from Andria*) 635—'Proximus sum egomet mihi' ('I am closest to myself').

4 *A priori*: Latin: from what comes before. Technical term in philosophy. An a priori proposition is one which can be known to be true or false without reference to experience. Nietzsche is referring implicitly and ironically to Kant, who argued that a priori concepts are presupposed by the very possibility of experience (*Critique of Pure Reason*, 1781). The Nietzschean sense of a priori here is that of the basic assumptions or convictions which motivate an argument.

'half children's games and half God at heart': quotation from Goethe, *Faust*, i. 3781.

5 *categorical imperative*: technical term from Kantian philosophy. In the *Critique of Practical Reason* (1788), Kant identifies two forms of moral imperative—the hypothetical and the categorical. The hypothetical imperative is binding only under certain conditions and takes the form of an 'if . . . , then . . .' structure. The categorical imperative is universally binding and is closely related to Kant's insistence on the universalizability of the structures and principles of the rational individual subject. According to Kant, one should perform only those actions from which a universally valid principle can be inferred.

Dr Paul Rée: Paul Rée (1849–1901), German writer on ethics and close friend of Nietzsche. Author of *The Origin of Moral Sensations* (1877). Influenced by empiricist psychology and Utilitarian ethics. See note to p. 11 below, on English psychologists.

7 *Schopenhauer*: Arthur Schopenhauer (1788–1860), German philosopher. Author of *The World as Will and Representation* (1818/

1844), he was, along with Wagner, the major early influence on Nietzsche. Instrumental in introducing Eastern ideas into the Western philosophical tradition, he held that human desire and will is doomed to frustration and that serenity can be attained only through the self-cancellation of the will. This conviction forms the basis of his ethics.

7 *sinister*: in German: *unheimlich*. *Unheimlich* may also mean 'uncanny', the standard translation of the term as it is used by Freud in his essay 'The Uncanny' (*Das Unheimliche*) (1919). For Freud, the specific sense of the uncanny is the disturbing yet strangely familiar effect of the return of the repressed. In contrast, Nietzsche's use of the term is less accented and implies no similar theoretical framework. None the less, *unheimlich* is consistently used to describe the disguised forms assumed by the will to power of *ressentiment* and might be construed in terms of a return of the repressed. However, as Nietzsche's argument makes clear, the will to power is less repressed *by* than differently expressed *through ressentiment*. Accordingly, *unheimlich* is translated as 'sinister' throughout. On *ressentiment*, see note to p. 22; on the will to power, see note to p. 58.

Buddhism: eastern religion of self-abnegation. Buddhism was a major influence on Schopenhauer through its central concept of *nirvana*, the state of serenity consequent upon the renunciation of all worldly desire.

nihilism: literally, the belief in nothing (from Latin: *nihil*). A vague or floating term in the late nineteenth century, closely associated with the cultural discourse on decadence, it was first introduced into this context by the Russian writer Turgenev in his novel *Fathers and Sons* (1861). Broadly, nihilism designates radical loss of belief and implies destructive action as a result. Nietzsche's decisive innovation is to identify nihilism with supposedly positive movements such as Christianity and socialism.

Plato . . . Kant: Nietzsche refers to the following philosophers in sequence: Plato (427–347 BC); Baruch de Spinoza (1632–77); François de La Rochefoucauld (1613–80); Immanuel Kant (1724–1804). He may be alluding to the following works respectively: *Republic* 606a–606b; *Ethica more geometrico demonstrata*, §50; *Réflexions ou Sentences et Maximes Morales*, §264; *Critique of Practical Reason*.

8 *Tartufferie*: hypocrisy, with reference to the play *Tartuffe* (1664) by the French comic dramatist Molière. The protagonist is a religious hypocrite.

9 *Darwin*: Charles Darwin (1809–82), English naturalist, author of *The Origin of Species* (1859) and *The Descent of Man* (1871), best-known for his theory of evolution as determined by the 'survival of the fittest'.

gay science: allusion to Nietzsche's work of 1882 entitled *The Gay Science*.

Dionysian drama: Dionysus is a central figure/concept in Nietzsche's work. In Greek mythology and religion, the god of wine and patron of drama, he first appears in Nietzsche's work in *The Birth of Tragedy* (1872) in conjunction with the complementary figure/concept of Apollo. According to Nietzsche, while Apollo represents the control, form and structure of individuated identity, Dionysus stands for the intoxication of the unstructured and chaotic flux which precedes individuation. In Nietzsche's later work (e.g. *The Antichrist*, 1888), the figure of Apollo is eclipsed, and the central opposition becomes one between Christ and Dionysus, between the denial and affirmation of life as it is, with all its pain and injustice.

my 'Zarathustra': Reference to *Thus Spake Zarathustra* (1883–5).

10 *rumination*: Nietzsche's positive view of rumination here contrasts with his critique of rumination as living in the past at the expense of the present in his second *Untimely Meditation*, *On the Use and Disadvantage of History* (1874), §1.

11 *English psychologists*: this is an umbrella term which Nietzsche uses to designate empiricist psychology (Locke), Utilitarian ethics (Mill and Bentham), and the evolutionary theory of development (Darwin), all associated in his view with the science and scholarship of Victorian England. Specific figures mentioned later in the text include Herbert Spencer and Henry Buckle. The representative of similar ideas in Germany is, for Nietzsche, Paul Rée.

partie honteuse: French: shameful side, aspect.

vis inertiae: Latin: force of inertia.

Christianity (and Plato): according to Nietzsche, Christianity inherits the Platonic tendency to privilege the transcendent over the immanent, the ideal over the real, and thus depreciates the present life. As will become clear, Nietzsche considers Judaism, socialism, and feminism equally transcendentalizing and destructive.

12 *pathos of distance*: Nietzsche's term for the difference between the noble and the servile, referring both to differences in social status

and values. First introduced in *Beyond Good and Evil* (1886), §257, the term recurs later in *Twilight of the Idols* (1888), 'Expeditions of an Untimely Man', §37. It recurs within the present text in III §14. While Nietzsche's main argument seems to be that the pathos of distance should at least be maintained if not intensified, he also suggests that the external difference in values which it represents may be internalized as the mark of a 'higher nature' (I §16), a development which considerably complicates the apparently straightforward opposition.

13 *désintéressé*: French: disinterested. An allusion to the Kantian postulation of disinterested and universal ethical principles.

14 *Herbert Spencer*: (1820–1903), English philosopher, psychologist and sociologist. Anticipating Darwin, Spencer combined evolutionary theory with Utilitarianism in his analysis of ethics. On this basis, that which preserves or is useful to life is deemed good.

etymological perspective: the etymological investigation of ethical terms is central to Nietzsche's genealogy of morals. Typically, Nietzsche uses etymology to trace the 'original' meaning of ethical vocabulary and thus provide 'historical' support for his assertion of the priority of noble over slave morality. As a result, Nietzsche's etymologies are often speculative and tendentious.

schlecht... schlicht... schlechtweg, schlechterdings...: Nietzsche's etymology is, in this instance, correct.

15 *Thirty Years War*: European-wide religious war (1618–48), fuelled by antagonism between Protestants and Catholics and Habsburg expansionist ambitions.

Buckle: Henry Thomas Buckle (1821–62), English cultural historian, author of *History of Civilization* (1857), which sought to establish the laws of history on a positivist basis.

arya: Sanscrit for 'Aryan'.

Theognis: Greek poet (*c*.500 BC), the subject of an article written by Nietzsche while still a student.

16 *esthlos*: Greek: good; brave, stout; noble; well-bred; morally good, faithful; fortunate, lucky.

kakos: Greek: ugly; ill-born; craven, base; worthless; sorry, unskilled; evil; wretched; pernicious; unlucky.

deilos: Greek: cowardly; vile, worthless; low-born, mean; miserable, wretched.

agathos: Greek: good; well-born, gentle; aristocrat; brave, valiant; capable; morally good; serviceable.

malus: Latin: bad, evil, wicked, injurious, destructive, mischievous, hurtful; ill-looking, ugly, deformed; evil, unlucky.

melas: Greek: black, dark; swarthy; murky; indistinct; obscure, enigmatic; malignant.

'hic niger est': 'this really is a black soul', quotation from Horace, *Satires*, I. iv. 85.

Fin-Gal: Irish mythological hero of the third century BC. Father of Ossian.

Virchow: Rudolf Virchow (1821–1902), German cell pathologist and liberal politician. One of the founders of modern anthropology.

anarchism... European socialists... 'commune': here Nietzsche engages in a broad attack on nineteenth-century left-wing ideas. Anarchism is a body of ideas developed by the French thinker Pierre Joseph Proudhon and elaborated by the Russian Mikhail Bakunin. Essentially a radical political doctrine opposed to all forms of institutional power, anarchism sought to substitute a form of communal living based on direct democracy for the apparatus of the modern state. Although not dominated by anarchists, the Paris Commune of 1871 constituted a short-lived experiment in this kind of social organization. Nietzsche fails to distinguish between anarchism and socialism, whose primary aim in the nineteenth century was the creation of a classless society through the abolition of private property and the common ownership of the means of production. In focusing on the egalitarian ideal shared by both movements, Nietzsche ignores their divergence over the relative importance of the individual and the collective, over the role of the state, and over what constitutes appropriate or useful political action.

17 *bonus*: Latin: good.

bellum: Latin: war.

good... godly... Goths...: Nietzsche's use of etymology here is highly speculative.

18 *Weir Mitchell's isolation therapy*: Silas Weir Mitchell (1829–1914), American doctor and dietician. Author of *Fat and Blood* (1884).

hysteria: in the mid-nineteenth century, an ill-defined term for mental illness, associated predominantly with women. Hysteria was given its initial psychoanalytic definition as the neurotic symptomatization of repressed psychic material by Sigmund Freud and Josef Breuer in *Studies in Hysteria* (1895). On neurosis, see note to p. 120.

18 *fakirs and Brahmins—Brahman*: a fakir is a Hindu ascetic, while the Brahmins constitute the highest Indian caste, with a priestly function. According to the teaching of the Brahmins, the Brahma is the world-soul from which all worlds proceed.

unio mystica: Latin: mystical union.

nirvana: according to Buddhism, the ideal state of the extinction of the individual will, which can only be described negatively.

20 *who inherited this Jewish transvaluation*: i.e. Christ and Christianity. It is important to realize the extent to which Nietzsche indiscriminately identifies Platonism, Judaism, and Christianity as transcendentalizing doctrines which depreciate the actual life. Nietzsche is not anti-Semitic, but anti-idealist, anti-transcendentalist.

the slave revolt in morals: reference to Nietzsche's first use of the term in *Beyond Good and Evil*, §195.

21 *sub hoc signo*: Latin: under this sign. Reworking of the motto which the Christian Emperor Constantine I had inscribed on the cross, '*In hoc signo vinces*' ('in this sign you will triumph'). In Nietzsche's version, which changes the prefix and drops the verb of the original, the cross becomes a symbol of submissiveness rather than of future triumph.

Quaeritur: Latin: it is asked; the question poses itself.

22 *ressentiment*: French: resentment. A central concept in Nietzsche's argument, *ressentiment* is the essence of slave morality, a purely reactive mode of feeling which simply negates the active and spontaneous affirmation of values on the part of the nobility.

23 *in effigie*: Latin: in effigy, in the form of an image.

deilos . . . mochtheros: Greek terms; *deilos*: see above, note to p. 16; *delaios*: wretched, sorry, paltry; *poneros*: oppressed by toils; toilsome, painful, grievous; in sorry plight; injurious; worthless, knavish; base, cowardly; *mochtheros*: suffering hardship, knavish.

oizyros . . . xymphora: Greek terms; *oizyros*: woeful, miserable, toilsome; wretch; *anolbos*: unblessed, wretched, luckless, poor; *tlemon*: wretched, miserable; *dystychein*: to be unlucky, unfortunate; *xymphora*: misfortune.

eu prattein: Greek: to act well; to prosper.

24 *gennaios*: Greek: true to one's birth or descent; high-born, noble; well-bred; good, excellent.

Mirabeau: Honoré Gabriel de Riqueti, Comte de Mirabeau (1749–91). French politician and writer, president of the National Assembly in 1791.

'love of one's enemy': allusion to Matthew 5: 43–4—'Ye have heard that it hath been said, Thou shalt love thy neighbour, and hate thine enemy.—But I say unto you, Love your enemies, bless them that curse you, do good to them that hate you, and pray for them that despitefully use you, and persecute you.'

25 *inter pares*: Latin: among equals.

blond beast: one of Nietzsche's most notoriously misread images, the 'blond beast' refers to a predatory animal, probably a lion, metaphorically associated with the ruthless representatives of aristocratic morality. As the development of the passage makes clear, the image carries no specific racial connotations and is not a reference to supposed Aryan supremacy.

26 *Pericles*: Athenian politician and orator of fifth century BC. On the funeral address, see Thucydides, *History of the Peloponnesian War*, 2. 41.

rhathymia: Greek: frivolity, carelessness.

now once again: reference to the Franco-Prussian War (1870) and the subsequent unification of Germany.

Hesiod's ... gold, silver, and bronze: Hesiod, Greek poet of *c.*700 BC, author of the *Theogony*, in which he distinguishes between three ages of history in declining order—the Golden, Silver, and Bronze. For Nietzsche's earlier comments on Hesiod, see *Daybreak*, §189.

27 *heroes and demigods of Troy and Thebes*: allusion to the figures of Homeric epic (Troy) and of Greek tragedy (Thebes is the setting for the Oedipus myth dramatized by Aeschylus and Sophocles).

28 *beyond good and evil*: reference to title of Nietzsche's work of 1886.

29 *'subject'*: in grammar, the part of speech of which something is predicated; in epistemology, the ground of knowledge, the knowing subject.

30 *atom*: according to the physicist Ernst Mach (1836–1916), the atom was an ideal mental construct rather than something which really existed.

Kantian 'thing in itself': reference to Kant's distinction in the *Critique of Pure Reason* between phenomenal appearance (*Erscheinung*) and noumenal essence (*Ding an sich*). According to Kant, the essence or thing in itself is beyond human knowledge, which is limited to phenomenal appearance.

31 *'for they know not what they do'*: Luke 23: 34—'Then said Jesus, Father, forgive them; for they know not what they do.'

33 *'I too was wrought by eternal love'*: loose quotation from Dante's *Divine Comedy* (*Inferno*, iii. 5–6): 'Fecemi la divina potestate, | La somma sapienza e 'l primo amore' ('I was created by the divine power, the highest wisdom and the primal love'). Inscription over the gates of Hell.

Thomas Aquinas: (1225–74), medieval theologian and philosopher.

'Beati... complaceat': 'The blessed in the kingdom of heaven will see the punishment of the damned so that they may enjoy their bliss all the more.' Loose quotation of Aquinas's *Summa Theologicae*, III, *Supplementum*, Q.94, Art. 1.

Church Father: Tertullian (*c.*150–225 AD).

this delighted visionary...: the long quotation which follows is from Tertullian, 'On Spectacles', in Revd Alexander Roberts and James Donaldson (eds.), *Translations of the Writings of the Fathers*, vol. 11, *The Writings of Tertullian*, vol. 1 (Edinburgh: T.&T. Clark, 1869), 8–35 (translation slightly altered). 'Yes, and there are other sights: that last day of judgement with its everlasting issues; that day unlooked for by the nations, the theme of their derision, when the world hoary with age and all its many products, shall be consumed in one great flame! How vast a spectacle then bursts upon the eye! *What there excites my admiration? what my derision? Which sight gives me joy? which rouses me to exultation?*—as I see so many illustrious monarchs, whose reception into the heavens was publicly announced, groaning now in the lowest darkness with Jupiter [my trans.] himself, and those too who bore witness of their exultation; governors of provinces, too, who persecuted the Christian name, in fires more fierce than those with which in the days of their pride they raged against the followers of Christ. What world's wise men besides, the very philosophers, in fact, who taught their followers that God had no concern in aught that is sublunary, and were wont to assure them that either they had no souls, or that they would never return to the bodies which at death they had left, now covered with shame before the poor deluded ones, as one fire consumes them! Poets also, trembling not before the judgement-seat of Rhadamanthus or Minos, but of the unexpected Christ! I shall have a better opportunity then of hearing the tragedians, louder-voiced in their own calamity; of viewing the play-actors, much more "dissolute" in the dissolving flame; of looking upon the charioteer, all glowing in his chariot of fire; of beholding the wrestlers, not in their gymnasia, but tossing in the fiery billows; unless even then I shall not care to attend to such ministers of sin, in my eager wish rather to fix a gaze *insatiable* on those whose fury vented itself against the Lord. "This", I shall say, "this is that carpenter's or hireling's son [*quaestuaria* means 'prostitute', not 'hireling'—*my note*], that sabbath-breaker, that Samaritan and devil-possessed! This is He whom you purchased from Judas! This is He whom you struck with reed and fist, whom you contemptuously spat upon, to whom you gave gall and vinegar to drink! This is He whom his disciples stole secretly away, that it might be said that He had risen again, or the gardener abstracted, that his lettuces might come to no harm from the crowds of visitants!" What quaestor or priest in his munificence will bestow on you the favour of seeing and *exulting in such things as these*? And yet even now we in a measure have them *by faith* in the picturings of imagination. But what are the things which eye has not seen, ear has not heard, and which have not so much as dimly dawned upon the human heart? Whatever they are, they are nobler, I believe, than circus and both theatres, and every race-course.'

34 *Rhadamanti... Minois*: Rhadamanthus and Minos, in Greek myth, were brothers and kings of Crete. After their death both were appointed judges in the Underworld.

Talmud: the most important post-biblical body of teaching, law, and interpretation in the Judaic tradition.

per fidem: Latin: truly. Also pun on *perfid*, German for perfidious.

35 *stood convicted... mankind*: quotation from Tacitus, *Annals*, xv. 14.

however much literary forgery... to bring it about: allusion to the questionable attribution of the Gospel of St John and the Book of Revelation to the same author.

36 *... Napoleon*: This section of Nietzsche's argument applies his analysis of aristocratic and slave moralities to the interpretation of some of the major shifts in modern European history. As a return to the aristocratic classical tradition displaced and suppressed by medieval Christianity, the Renaissance represented one of Nietzsche's cultural ideals. The Protestant Reformation, however, was in his view one of the most disastrous examples of the slave revolt in morals, while the overthrow of the French mon-

archy and aristocracy marked a further decisive step in the progress of slave morality towards hegemony. Occurring against the grain of historical development, the advent of Napoleon represented for Nietzsche a happy throwback to an earlier age of aristocratic morality where energy and ambition ruled.

37 *placed 'ad acta'*: Latin: 'laid to rest'.

38 *physiological investigation and interpretation*: together with etymology, physiology constitutes one of the main methodological resources for Nietzsche's genealogy of morals. The absolutes of slave morality are relativized through an appeal to history and the body.

39 *vis inertiae*: See above, note to p. 10.

'psychic assimilation': in German, *Einverseelung*. Nietzsche coined the word by analogy with *Einverleibung*, the German for 'incorporation' (translated here as 'physical assimilation').

tabula rasa: Latin: blank slate, tablet. Image used by the English empiricist John Locke to describe the mind prior to the imprint of sense impressions.

46 *twelve-table legislation of Rome*: in 450 BC the Roman Senate formulated a set of laws intended to supersede the existing common law. The new laws were inscribed on twelve bronze tablets in the Forum.

si plus minusve secuerunt, ne fraude esto: quotation from the sixth paragraph of the third tablet—'If they have cut off more or less, let that be no crime.'

faire le mal pour le plaisir de le faire: French: doing evil for the pleasure of it. Quotation from Prosper Mérimée, *Lettres à une inconnue* (1874).

47 *sympathia malevolens*: Latin: malevolent sympathy.

something... spiritual and 'divine': in German, *Vergeistigung* and '*Vergöttlichung*' respectively.

auto-da-fé: Portuguese: act of faith. Publication of the judgement passed on heretics by the Spanish Inquisition, and by extension, the public burning of heretics.

48 *Don Quixote at the court of the Duchess*: in the Second Part of Cervantes's *Don Quixote* (1615), the hero is made the butt of a series of sometimes brutal practical jokes while staying at the court of a duke and duchess.

Pope Innocent III: held office from 1198 to 1216, the highpoint of the political power of the medieval Church. Author of *De miseria humanae conditionis* (1195), whose main thesis Nietzsche summarizes here.

49 *Negroes*: German: *die Neger*. Nietzsche's terminology and views here are clearly racist, assuming an evolutionary difference between white European and black African.

sublimate and refine itself: in German, *Sublimierung* and *Subtilisierung* respectively. Nietzsche's use of metaphors drawn from chemical analysis dates from *Human All Too Human* (1878), *On the First and Last Things*, §1. His understanding of the alteration and refinement of instinctual drives anticipates Freud's notion of sublimation as the basis of culture.

les nostalgies de la croix: French: nostalgia for the cross.

50 *Calvin and Luther*: Nietzsche is referring to the fact that both Luther and Calvin resorted to violent means in order to consolidate the Reformation.

'Hercules of duty': allusion to Hercules' choice of virtue over pleasure, as related in Xenophon's *Memorabilia*. The episode, known as 'Hercules at the Crossroads', became a familiar Stoic commonplace.

51 *manas*: Veda Sanscrit: consciousness.

52 *Elend, êlend*: Nietzsche is relating the modern German word meaning 'misery' (*Elend*) to its etymological precursor in Middle High German (*êlend*), meaning 'abroad', 'foreign', 'banishment'.

the criminal is above all someone who 'breaks' ... breaks his word: Nietzsche here is punning on the cognate forms of *Verbrecher* (criminal) and *brechen* (to break).

53 *mimus*: Latin: image, imitation.

Vae victis!: Latin: Woe to the defeated. Quotation from the Roman historian Livy, *Ab Urbe Condita*, v. xlviii. 9.

compositio: Latin: comparison; amicable settlement of legal case. Technical term from Roman law.

54 *cancelling itself out ... self-cancellation*: in German, *sich selbst aufhebend* and *Selbstaufhebung*. *Aufheben* is ambiguous in German and may mean either to suppress or to preserve. The Hegelian concept of *Aufhebung*, the dialectical sublation of opposites which both cancels and conserves its constitutive terms, plays on both meanings. In Nietzsche, the consistent emphasis is on the sense of cancellation or suppression and no allusion to Hegel seems intended. On Hegel, see note to p. 85, where the philosopher appears explicitly in the text.

anti-Semites: Nietzsche was vehemently opposed to organized anti-Semitism, which he regarded as a product of *ressentiment*.

54 *retroactively*: in German, *nachträglich*. *Ressentiment* operates primarily in the mode of retroactivity, positing its derived values as original once the aristocratic values of the nobility have been discredited through the slave revolt in morals. There are similarities with Freud's notion of retroactivity, developed in the case-history of 'The Wolf-Man', *From the History of an Infantile Neurosis* (1918), whereby a neurosis can generate its own traumatic origin through phantasmatic desire.

55 *E. Dühring*: Eugen Karl Dühring (1833–1921), philosopher and political economist. Author of *The Value of Life* (1867) and *The Course of Philosophy* (1875), *Natural Dialectic* (1865), *Critical History of National Economy and Socialism* (1871), *Philosophy of Reality* (1878), *The Replacement of Religion through Perfection and the Elimination of Judaism through the Modern Spirit of Peoples* (1882). Dühring defended a positivist, mechanistic view of evolution determined by teleological ends. In his autobiography, *The Cause, My Life and Enemies* (1882), he claimed to be the founder of anti-Semitism. Attacked by Friedrich Engels in his *Anti-Dühring* (1878).

the aforementioned agitator: i.e. Dühring. The following quotation is from *The Cause, My Life and Enemies* (1882), a book found in Nietzsche's library.

56 *reactive and retroactive feelings*: in German, *Gegen- und Nach-Gefühle*. See note on *retroactively*, p. 54 above.

57 *causa fiendi*: Latin: initial cause, origin. Opposite of *causa finalis*, final cause.

58 *will to power*: a central concept in Nietzsche's work, the immanent principle of domination and appropriation which informs all life, even that which appears to oppose it. This discussion of the concept (II §12) is one of the clearest in Nietzsche's writings.

progressus: Latin: progress, advance.

the 'meaning' of the individual organs also changes: Nietzsche's insistence on the body's potential for reorganization implicitly questions the status he elsewhere ascribes it, that of an absolute ground for a physiological critique of values. See Nietzsche's note to the First Essay.

59 *misarchism*: neologism meaning: hatred of power or mastery (from Greek: *missein*, to hate; *archein*, to rule).

Huxley: Thomas Henry Huxley (1825–95), English biologist and supporter of Darwin, whose ideas he helped popularize.

60 *per analogiam*: Latin: by analogy.

all concepts in which a whole process is summarized in signs escape definition; only that which is without history can be defined: an assertion which raises the question of the viability of Nietzsche's etymological method of analysis as a quest for the origins of ethics. See above, note to p. 14.

62 *instrumentum*: Latin: instrument.

63 *Kuno Fischer*: (1824–1907), professor of philosophy at Heidelberg, author of a ten-volume *History of Modern Philosophy* (1865), which was one of Nietzsche's sources on Spinoza.

morsus conscientiae: Latin: pangs of conscience.

sub ratione boni: Latin: from the perspective of the good.

gaudium: Latin: joy.

66 *Heraclitus' 'great child'*: Heraclitus (*c*.544–483 BC), Presocratic philosopher. Nietzsche is alluding to Fragment 94: 'Lifetime is a child at play, moving pieces in a game. Kingship belongs to the child', trans. Charles H. Kahn, *The Art and Thought of Heraclitus* (1979).

'contract': allusion to contract theory in politics, according to which the state originates and derives its legitimacy from an agreement between consenting individuals. Closely associated with the thought of Jean-Jacques Rousseau (*The Social Contract*, 1762) and other intellectual precursors of the French Revolution. Although Nietzsche presents his own account of the genesis of the state as opposed to contract theory, which he identifies with *ressentiment* and slave morality, his insistence on the importance of the relationship between debtor and creditor is itself an emphasis on a contractual relation. However, whereas Rousseau stresses the equality between contracting partners, Nietzsche concentrates on the inequality (and power relation) between debtor and creditor.

67 *'labyrinth of the breast', to use Goethe's words*: quotation from Goethe's poem 'To the Moon' (*An den Mond*).

70 *mimicry*: in English in original.

71 *causa prima*: Latin: first cause.

74 *Aegisthos*: in Greek mythology, the incestuous son of Thyestes and his daughter Pelopeia. Aegisthos killed his stepfather Atreus

and took control of Mycene. Driven out by Agamemnon, he returned to seduce his wife Clytemnestra during the Trojan War, murdered Agamemnon on his return, and was killed by Agamemnon's son Orestes. The following quotation is from the *Odyssey*, i. 32–4.

76 *this Antichristian*: the German *Antichrist* may mean either Antichrist or Antichristian. Here, preceding Antinihilist, it seems more likely to mean the latter. Nietzsche plays on the ambiguity (negative Messiah/opponent of Christianity) in the title of a subsequent work of 1888—*Der Antichrist* (*The Antichrist/ian*).

Zarathustra: central character of *Thus Spake Zarathustra*, Nietzsche's work of 1883–5, based on the Persian founder of Zoroastrianism. According to Nietzsche, Zoroaster was the first to introduce dualism (good/evil, immanence/transcendence) into religion, and will thus be the first to overcome them, in the guise of Zarathustra.

77 [Epigraph]: quotation from *Thus Spake Zarathustra*, I: 'On Reading and Writing'. The figure of truth or wisdom as a woman is common in Nietzsche's later works. See the Preface to *Beyond Good and Evil*.

morbidezza: Italian: softness, sickliness.

novissima gloriae cupido: Latin: the most recent desire for fame. Allusion to Tacitus, *Histories*, iv. 6.

horror vacui: Latin: the horror of a vacuum; the dislike of empty space.

Richard Wagner: (1813–83), German composer. Along with Schopenhauer, the major early influence on Nietzsche. Nietzsche's first book *The Birth of Tragedy* (1872) is in part an argument for the regeneration of German culture through Wagner's opera, an ambitious synthesis of music and drama in a total work of art. In the fourth of the *Untimely Meditations*, *Richard Wagner in Bayreuth* (1875/6), Nietzsche begins to move to a more critical position, which intensifies considerably in *The Wagner Case* and *Nietzsche contra Wagner* (both 1888). Nietzsche's criticism of Wagner relates chiefly to the theatricality and religiosity of his later work.

78 *Luther's wedding*: subject of a projected drama by Wagner which was never completed.

Meistersinger: *Die Meistersinger von Nürnberg* (*The Mastersingers of Nuremburg*, 1868), Wagnerian opera.

Hafis: Muhammad Schamsaddin (1330–89), Persian poet. He was adopted by Goethe as a persona in his collection of poems, the *West-Östlicher Divan* (*West–East Divan*, 1815).

79 *Parsifal*: eponymous hero of Wagner's opera of 1882, based on Wolfram von Eschenbach's *Parzival* (*c.*1210). Parsifal, having spent his childhood in seclusion in a forest, frees King Amfortas from the spell of diabolic sorcerer Klingsor through the power of compassion.

satyr play: in ancient Greece, the performance of tragedies at the Dionysian festivals was followed by the performance of a comic satyr play.

spiritualization and sensualization: in German, *Vergeistigung* and *Versinnlichung* respectively.

80 *Feuerbach*: Ludwig Feuerbach (1804–72), German philosopher, a left Hegelian and precursor of Marx. In *The Essence of Christianity* (1841), Feuerbach interprets the concept of God in terms of the projection and alienation of human self-consciousness and potential.

'young Germans': name given by Imperial Edict of 1835 to a loosely identified group of left-liberal dissidents who opposed the reactionary political Establishment in Germany in the aftermath of the French Revolution of 1830.

contiguity: in English in the original. A technical term from associationist psychology, where the spatial metaphor of proximity is used to describe associative connections.

82 *milk of human, imperially human kindness*: allusion to Lady Macbeth's speech in Shakespeare's *Macbeth*, I. v.

Herwegh: Georg Herwegh (1815–75), German poet. Like Wagner, he participated in the 1848 uprisings in Germany and subsequently went into exile in Switzerland, where he introduced the composer to the work of Schopenhauer.

in majorem musicae gloriam: Latin: to the greater glory of music. Modelled on the stock religious formula *in majorem Dei gloriam* (to the greater glory of God). A reference to the privileged place occupied by music in Schopenhauer's philosophy as a result of its capacity to circumvent the phenomenal world and offer direct access to the underlying will.

83 *Kantian version of the aesthetic problem*: in the *Critique of Judgement* (1790), Kant stresses the disinterestedness (§2) and universal validity (§6) of aesthetic judgement.

83 *Stendhal . . . une promesse de bonheur*: in the travel book *Rome, Naples et Florence* (1854), the French novelist Stendhal (pen-name of Henri Beyle, 1783–1842) describes art as 'a promise of happiness'.

le désintéressement: French: disinterestedness.

84 *Pygmalion*: in Greek mythology, a sculptor who falls in love with the statue of a woman he has made.

sense of touch!: reference to 'On the Sense of Touch', in Kant's *Anthropology from a Pragmatic Point of View* (1798).

originate from a generalization of that sexual experience: without using the term (which he uses elsewhere in a similar context), Nietzsche here sketches out a theory of what Freud was later to call sublimation, the channelling of libidinal energy into cultural activity. See above, note to p. 49.

Epicurus: Greek philosopher (342–270 BC), who developed the idea that all things come into and leave existence by virtue of the joining and separation of atoms. He is popularly associated with the hedonistic pursuit of pleasure, hence 'Epicureanism'.

wheel of Ixion: in Greek mythology, Ixion was punished for his outrages against gods and men by being bound to a constantly moving wheel and tortured by the Furies.

85 *instrumentum diaboli*: Latin: instrument of the devil.

Hegel: Georg Wilhelm Friedrich Hegel (1770–1831), German philosopher. Hegel proposed a theory of human history as the teleological development of absolute spirit towards full self-consciousness and immanence through a dialectical process of position, negation, and sublation (*Aufhebung*), whereby historical forces confront and transform each other. Schopenhauer attacked the theory.

86 *Cynics*: school of Greek philosophers founded by Antisthenes (444–368 BC) with the aim of developing a form of life independent of state and religion.

la bête philosophe: French: the philosophical animal, a pun on the dual meaning of *bête* (animal/stupid).

87 *Socrates . . . got married ironice*: Socrates (469–399 BC), Greek philosopher, was married to Xanthippe, who became the stereotype for a nagging wife; *ironice* is Latin: ironically, in an ironic manner.

Rahula: Veda Sanscrit for: fetter, chain. Nietzsche's source for these quotations is H. Oldenburg, *Buddha: His Life, his Teachings, his Community* (1881).

pereat mundus, fiat philosophia, fiat philosophus, fiam!: Latin: May the world perish, let there be philosophy, let there be the philosopher, let there be I!

88 *believe me!*: Nietzsche is referring obliquely to his own solitary life style here.

89 *Temple of Artemis*: Nietzsche is referring to a story about Heraclitus in Ephesus, from Diogenes Laertius, *Lives of the Eminent Philosophers*: 'He would retire to the Temple of Artemis and play at knuckle-bones with the boys; and when the Ephesians stood round him and looked on, "Why you rascals", he said, "are you astonished? Is it not better to do this than to take part in your civil life?"' (trans. R. D. Hicks).

piazza di San Marco: square in front of the Church of Saint Mark in Venice.

'Empire': *Reich* in German, an allusion to the recent unification of Germany under Bismarck.

91 *vigor*: Latin: strength.

cancelled out: *aufgehoben* in German.

transfigured... as a sexual stimulus: see above, notes to pp. 49 and 84.

physiology of aesthetics: on this subject, see also Nietzsche's final note to the First Essay, and *Nietzsche contra Wagner*, §1.

92 *'ephectic'*: hesitating. Ephectics (Greek: the hesitating ones) was the nickname given to the Sceptics, who were perceived as withholding their judgement on whatever issue was under discussion.

'sine ira et studio': Latin: with neither anger nor enthusiasm.

'nitimur in vetitum': Latin: we strive after what is forbidden. Quotation from Ovid, *Amores*, III. iv. 7.

hubris: Greek: overweening pride. In tragedy, the flaw which brings about the protagonist's downfall (nemesis).

Charles the Bold... Louis XI, 'je combats l'universelle araignée': Charles the Bold, Duke of Burgundy (1467–77), failed in his attempt to re-establish his duchy as a regional power-base against the centralizing ambitions of the French king Louis XI, of whom he said 'I am fighting the ever-present spider.'

93 *jus primae noctis*: Latin: right of the first night, the feudal right of the lord of the manor to deflower the bride of his serf.

vendetta: Italian: blood feud.

vetitum: Latin: what is forbidden.

94 *Vishvamitra*: mythical forefather of an ancient Indian family of priests. According to legend, he attained supernatural powers through ascetic self-discipline.

97 *crux, nux, lux*: Latin: 'cross, nut, light'. This is the Colli–Montinari text; earlier editions give '*crux, nox, lux*' (cross, night, light).

Vedanta: originally, the name for the *Upanishads*, the final section of holy scripture of *Veda* (Sanscrit for 'knowledge') which dates from 800 to 600 BC. Later, the name for the philosophy of Brahmanism. In contrast to the *Veda*, the *Vedanta* interprets life as a painful cycle of reincarnations from which the only escape is a renunciation of the world and a turning towards the absolute, Brahma.

'subject' and 'object': epistemological distinction between the knower and the known, the knowing subject and the object of knowledge.

98 *'intelligible character of things'*: reference to Kant's distinction between the phenomenal and the noumenal, the empirically perceptible and the rationally intelligible aspects of an object of knowledge. For Kant, the 'intelligible character of things' remains beyond the reach of empirically based knowledge.

102 *homines bonae voluntatis*: Latin: men of good will.

'beautiful souls': allusion to the section of Goethe's novel *Wilhelm Meister's, Apprenticeship* entitled 'Confessions of a Beautiful Soul'. The phrase carries ironic connotations of affected refinement. See also Hegel's *Phenomenology of Spirit*, 6 Cc.

Bogos: tribe of northern Ethiopia.

Pharisee: the Pharisees were a Jewish religious group criticized for hypocrisy by Christ thoughout the Gospels.

105 *in effigie*: see above, note to p. 73.

106 *nervus sympathicus*: part of the intestinal nervous system.

107 *'One thing is needful'*: Luke 10: 42. 'But one thing is needful: and Mary hath chosen that good part, which shall not be taken away from her.'

witch-trials: reference to medieval and early modern practice of trying and executing people assumed guilty of participating in witchcraft.

[causal interpretation]: these and the following square brackets in this section are Nietzsche's.

108 *materialism*: in philosophy, the opposite of idealism. The belief that reality is defined and determined by matter rather than ideas.

Materialism first emerged in the ancient world, then reappeared with the Enlightenment and reached its highpoint in the nineteenth century in opposition to the thought of German Idealism, particularly that of Hegel. Materialism has variously sought to ground itself in physics (Lucretius), evolutionary biology and psychology (Social Darwinism), and a developmental view of history (Marx). Although Nietzsche's thought incorporates elements of materialism, such as the emphasis on physiology, its determinism is ultimately incompatible with his voluntarism.

109 *Weltschmerz*: German: the pain of the world. Term coined by the German Romantic writer Jean Paul Richter (1763–1825) in his *Selina or On the Immortality of the Soul* (1804).

vegetarians: in English in the original.

Shakespeare's foolish knight Sir Andrew Aguecheek: allusion to Shakespeare *Twelfth Night*, I. iii, where Aguecheek remarks—'I am a great eater of beef, and I believe that does harm to my wit.' Nietzsche's text refers here not to Sir Andrew Aguecheek but to Junker Christoph (von Bleichenwang), the name given to Aguecheek in the German Schlegel/Tieck translation of *Twelfth Night*.

110 *Pascal's principle 'il faut s'abêtir'*: Blaise Pascal (1623–62), French religious philosopher and mathematician, stressed the limits of rational knowledge, hence the imperative 'one must become stupid'. See above, note to '*la bête philosophe*', p. 86.

sportsmen: in English in the original.

training: in English in the original.

Hesychasts of Mount Athos: monks of the Greek Orthodox Church, whose meditation is meant to induce mystic revelation of divine light.

St Theresa: Theresa of Avila (1515–82), Spanish mystic.

111 *commentary of Shankara ... Paul Deussen*: Deussen (1834–1919), a schoolfriend of Nietzsche, was the editor of Schopenhauer and translator of numerous Indian religious texts. Nietzsche relies on his *The System of the Vedânta* (1883) and quotes from his translation *The Sutras of the Vedânta* (1887). Nietzsche juxtaposes several passages from Deussen's translation of the commentary of Shankara, a theologian of the ninth or tenth century AD, in order to form a continuous whole.

unio mystica: See above, note to p. 78.

112 *Epicurus*: See above, note to p. 84. Despite his popular association with hedonism, Epicurus's atomism actually led him to

advocate imperturbability (the Greek *ataraxie*) as the highest virtue in face of the ephemeral nature of all things.

112 *Stoicism*: doctrine of the Stoics, a school of philosophers founded by Zenon of Kition around 300 BC. Its morality was based on the rational laws of nature, involving the unflinching acceptance of what they produced.

training: in English in the original.

incuria sui: Latin: indifference towards oneself, self-neglect.

113 *cénacle*: French: literary or intellectual circle.

Geulincx's 'despectio sui': Arnold Geulincx (1624–69), philosopher who developed the doctrine of occasionalism, whereby God synchronized the divergent realms of the physical and the spiritual through occasional intervention. The proper attitude of the individual in whose life this intervention was likely to occur was, therefore, 'contempt for oneself'.

115 *feminism... Idealism*: a further example of Nietzsche's tendency indiscriminately to identify what he regards as transcendentalizing doctrines. See above, notes to pp. 11 and 20.

dishonest lie: possible allusion to Plato's 'noble lie' in *Republic*, 414c.

116 *Lord Byron... Thomas Moore*: George Gordon Noel, Lord Byron (1788–1824), English Romantic poet. Thomas Moore (1779–1852), Irish poet, Byron's biographer.

Dr Gwinner: Wilhelm von Gwinner (1825–1917), author of *A Portrait of Schopenhauer from Personal Acquaintance* (1862).

'eis heauton': Greek: against himself.

Thayer: Alexander Wheelock Thayer (1817–97), American historian and biographer.

Jannsen: Johannes Janssen, author of *History of the German People since the Middle Ages* (1877).

Taine: Hyppolite Taine (1828–93), French historian and philosopher of history, who sought to interpret history in terms of the influence of environmental factors.

Leopold Ranke: German historian (1795–1886), who stressed the methodological importance of factual sources in an attempt to reconstruct history 'as it really happened'.

advocatus: Latin: advocate.

causa fortior: Latin: stronger cause.

117 *that diplomat*: allusion to Charles Maurice de Talleyrand (1754–1838), bishop of Autun before the French Revolution, and subsequently a senior diplomat under various regimes. A great survivor of French politics.

119 *'My kingdom is not of this world'*: John 18: 36.

Goethe... thirty-six tragic situations: see the *Conversations with Eckermann*, 14 Feb. 1830.

120 *training*: in English in the original.

Saint Vitus's and Saint John's dancers: both St Vitus and St John were associated as patrons with conditions such as epilepsy, hysteria, and possession.

'evviva la morte!': Italian: Long live death.

neurosis: *Neurose* in German. In the 1880s, a general term for psychological disturbance. First given a specific psychoanalytic definition (of physical symptoms induced by repression) eight years later by Sigmund Freud and Josef Breuer in their *Studies in Hysteria* (1895).

Quaeritur: see above, note to p. 21.

121 *magno sed proxima intervallo*: Latin: next in line, but by a long way.

in artibus et litteris: Latin: in arts and letters.

Salvation Army: English religious charitable organization, organized along military lines, set up by William Booth in 1865.

'Here I stand, I can do no other': at the Diet of Worms (1521), Luther's alleged reply to the request that he should recant his doctrines.

rococo: eighteenth-century style of art and decoration characterized by its lightness and delicacy. As an adjective, the term carries pejorative connotations of ridiculous over-elaboration.

122 *'the crown of eternal life'*: allusion to Revelations 2: 10: 'be thou faithful unto death, and I will give thee a crown of life.'

123 *non plus ultra*: Latin: what cannot be surpassed.

124 *the whole of our modern science*: 'unsere ganze moderne Wissenschaft' in German. *Wissenschaft* may refer to both natural sciences (*Naturwissenschaften*) and humanities (*Geisteswissenschaften*). In the extended discussion of 'science' which follows, Nietzsche seems at times to be referring to the natural sciences in general, and at others exclusively to contemporary positivist historiography, which sought to place the discipline of history on a scientific basis. As a result, certain passages are ambiguous.

125 *despectio sui*: see above, note to p. 113.

126 *Assassins*: both the crusaders and their Saracen antagonists were terrorized by the members of the secret society of the Assassins, based in Persia and Syria, founded by Hasan-ben-Sabbah, 'the Old Man of the Mountain'.

secretum: Latin: secret.

labyrinth . . . Minotaur: in Greek mythology, the Cretan Minotaur, half-man and half-bull, was confined in a labyrinth designed by Daedalus. Theseus killed the monster and escaped from the labyrinth with the help of Ariadne, the daughter of the Cretan king Minos. The motif of Ariadne and the labyrinth recurs in Nietzsche's late work and letters, where it becomes associated with the figure of Dionysus. In one variation of the myth, Ariadne takes Dionysus as her lover after being abandoned by Theseus.

127 *factum brutum . . . 'petits faits' . . . petit faitalisme*: Latin: brute fact; French: little facts; pun on French *fait* (fact) and *fatalisme* (fatalism) Nietzsche considered the fact-based philosophy of positivism a form of fatalism, a kind of acquiescence in the continuation of the *status quo*.

129 *'poor in spirit'*: allusion to Matthew 5: 3 'Blessed are the poor in spirit: for theirs is the kingdom of heaven.'

130 *theological astronomy*: the Ptolemaic view of the universe as centred on the earth, which was accepted by medieval theology.

Copernicus: Nicolas Copernicus (1473–1543), astronomer who replaced the earlier geocentric model of the universe with a heliocentric one.

Kant . . . 'it annihilates my importance': in the *Critique of Practical Reason* (1788), Kant notes how the view of the night sky relativizes the status of the individual which his philosophy then seeks to re-establish through the theory of innate moral law. A possible allusion to the celebrated opening sentence of the Conclusion: 'Two things fill the mind with ever new and increasing admiration and awe, the oftener and more steadily we reflect on them: *the starry heavens above and the moral law within*.'

ataraxie: Greek: imperturbability.

Kant's victory over the conceptual dogma of theology: in the *Critique of Pure Reason* (1781) Kant criticized the listed concepts as ideas lacking any objective content.

131 *Xaver Doudan*: Ximénès Doudan (1800–82), French writer and politician.

131 *'ravages' caused by 'l'habitude ... dans l'inconnu'*: French for: ravages caused by 'the custom of admiring the unintelligible instead of simply remaining in the unknown'.

elegantia syllogismi: Latin: elegance of argument.

'Nada!': Spanish: nothing!

metapolitics of St Petersburg: reference to Pan-Slavism and the developing sense of a Russian national mission in the late nineteenth century.

Tolstoyan 'compassion': Leo Nicolayevich, Count Tolstoy (1828–1910). Russian novelist, who from 1882 developed unorthodox Christian ideas and adopted a life-style modelled on that of the peasantry.

132 *species anarchista*: Latin: the anarchist kind.

Renan: Ernest Renan (1823–92), French historian of religion. Author of *Vie de Jésus* (1863). He attempted to reconcile Christian doctrine with a positivist approach to the study of biblical history.

Fates: in Greek mythology the Fates decided the time of death of mortals by cutting the threads of their life with shears. Here, however, the reference is to castration.

Anacreontic: reference to the *Anacreonta*, a collection of poems purportedly in the style of the Greek poet Anacreon (*c*.500 BC). Ode 24 begins: 'Nature gave horns to bulls, hooves to horses, fleetness of foot to hares, to lions an abyss of teeth (*chasm' odonton*)...'

Tartufferie: see above, note to p. 8.

133 *Deutschland, Deutschland über alles*: first line of the *Lied der Deutschen* (1841) by August Heinrich Hoffmann von Fallersleben (1798–1874). From 1922, it was the German national anthem.

paralysis agitans: Parkinson's disease.

la religion de la souffrance: French: the religion of suffering.

134 *work in progress: The Will to Power: An Attempt at a Transvaluation of all Values*: the projected work of that title was eventually abandoned by Nietzsche. The existing text of *The Will to Power* (1901/6) is a collection of fragments put together posthumously by Nietzsche's sister, Elisabeth Förster-Nietzsche, and his friend Heinrich Köselitz (Peter Gast). Its editorial integrity is suspect.

Sankhya philosophy: Sankhya is one of the oldest writings of the Brahmanic tradition. It systematizes the doctrines of the religion.

135 *self-cancellation . . . 'self-overcoming'*: *Selbstaufhebung* and *Selbstüberwindung* respectively in German.

'patere legem, quam ipse tulisti': Latin: submit to the law which you yourself have decreed.

136 *'faute de mieux'*: French: for want of something better.

INDEX